FRONTLINE
AFGHANISTAN

British Army driver Private Matt 'Pimmy' Pimblett with his Mastiff Armoured Battlefield ambulance.

FRONTLINE AFGHANISTAN

THE DEVIL'S PLAYGROUND

MIKE RYAN

SPELLMOUNT

This book is dedicated to all the brave men and women of our armed forces and those of our NATO allies, as they battle for the freedom and liberty of the Afghan people in order to release both them and us from the bloody threat of terrorism.

First published 2010

Spellmount Publishers, The History Press
The Mill, Brimscombe Port
Stroud, Gloucestershire, GL5 2QG
www.thehistorypress.co.uk

© Mike Ryan, 2010

The right of Mike Ryan to be identified as the Author
of this work has been asserted in accordance with the
Copyrights, Designs and Patents Act 1988.

British Library Cataloguing in Publication Data.
A catalogue record for this book is available from the British Library.

ISBN 978 0 7524 5248 7

Typesetting and origination by The History Press
Printed in Great Britain

CONTENTS

	Author's Appeal	8
	Acknowledgements	9
	Author's Note	9
	Introduction	12
I	The Crucible of Terrorism	16
II	Wild Frontiers	24
III	Learning From the Bears	32
IV	Dodging the Golden BB	40
V	Bullet Magnets	48
VI	The Reapers	60
VII	The Golden Hour	69
VIII	The Devil's Playground	77
IX	Combat Sitrep	113
X	Final Thoughts	176
XI	The Fallen	180
	Military Fatalities by Country	208
	Abbreviations	209
	Afterword by Myrdal Mya	213
	Index	222

US Marines taking 5. In July
2009 4,000 Marines poured
into southern Afghanistan's
Helmand province. 'Where we
go we will stay and where we
stay we will hold, build and
work toward transition of all
security responsibilities to
Afghan forces.' (Marine Corps
Brig.Gen Larry Nicholson.)

AUTHOR'S APPEAL

At the time of writing this book British casualties in Afghanistan are running at almost one a day, and like many statistics this does not tell the full story, nor indeed show the tragedy that is behind each and every fatality or injury. Those with superficial wounds are often back in action within days of being injured, for others that is sadly not the case. I am of course referring to all those who have been seriously wounded and whose injuries are so severe that they will not return to normal life quickly – if at all.

Their plight is particularly hard to come to terms with, as by nature they are young and fit individuals who were, prior to being wounded, physically and mentally ready for almost anything. They are as you can imagine extremely brave people, whose only wish is to put their lives back together so that they can go on living a useful and fulfilling life without being a burden on society. And they need our help to do this.

Whilst our medical and rehabilitation care is truly excellent, it is what happens beyond this stage of recovery that needs more support – and this is where you can help.

The following charities and organisations do fantastic work with our service personnel and their families, and I am sure that they would be extremely grateful for any help or donation that you can give.

www.helpforheroes.org.uk
www.ssafa.org.uk
www.armybenfund.org
www.blesma.org

Thank you for your kindness.

Mike Ryan

ACKNOWLEDGEMENTS

I would like to thank the following individuals, organisations and companies for their kind help in supporting me with the research and production of this book. Shaun Barrington of The History Press for his enthusiasm and support, Peter Robinson MA, John Ryan, Jackhammer, RMAS, BCMH, UK MoD, US DoD, Australian DoD, Canadian DoD, Avpro Aerospace and all the soldiers and aircrew who kindly donated their time to tell their stories.

Also special thanks to my good friend Myrdal Mya for his thoughts on Afghanistan's future. Thanks also to my wife Fiona, and children, Isabella, Angelina and Jamie for their patience and understanding during my various times away from home interviewing and researching.

Photo credits: special thanks to the UK Ministry of Defence, Australian DoD, Canadian DoD, US DoD, Avpro Aerospace, SOCOM, Haymarket Publishing, *Camouflage* magazine and everyone else who kindly donated imagery. Every effort has been made to acknowledge copyright. If there are any omissions, the publishers apologise and undertake to correct on reprint.

Author's Note

Please note for operational security (OPSEC) reasons, certain tactical, technical and operational procedural details have either been changed or omitted in order to protect the security and welfare of both our armed forces and those of our allies operating in Afghanistan, as military operations in this region of the world are likely to be ongoing for many years to come.

Above, top to bottom:

British convoy on its way to a new FOB.

President Obama having a heart to heart with General Stanley McChrystal as to the best way forward in Afghanistan.

USMC MV 22B Osprey taking off for Camp Bastion, Afghanistan. This is one of 10 Ospreys currently being deployed in support of Operation Enduring Freedom.

US Marines on sweep and clear mission.

INTRODUCTION

Four years ago, I wrote a book called *Battlefield Afghanistan*. It was at the time of its publication the only book on the market that told the real story of what was going in that troubled country at the height of the bloody summer of 2006, as British soldiers fought contact after contact against their tenacious enemy, the Taliban. Why this should have been the case is puzzling as there were certainly enough journalists and commentators to tell the story, and yet they did not. Perhaps the lure of covering the war in Iraq was stronger; or could it have been that the war had been so played down that most thought we had won it and everyone had gone home?

I too would have been lulled into a false sense of what was happening in Afghanistan were it not for one thing. I knew many soldiers who were serving out there, and their harrowing accounts made me realise that all was not well and that there was a story to be told. I of course was not alone in these sentiments, as a number of senior officers in the British Army also felt that the real story of what was going on in Afghanistan needed to be told, and told quickly as the situation in some areas of the British controlled AOP (area of operations) was nearing meltdown.

When writing *Battlefield Afghanistan*, I decided from the outset not just to cover the war stories, as I anticipated many books appearing eventually that would either cover major military operations in some detail or alternatively the actions of specific units involved in them. Instead, I decided to make my book more of a tactical guide – aimed in part at soldiers about to go out on operations in Afghanistan who prior to their deployment knew either little or nothing about the long and complicated history of the country they were about to fight in.

You would have thought that their pre-deployment work-up training would have given them the information that they needed, but that was not always the case. At the present time, there are a number of NATO forces that have that book on reading lists for all soldiers before they deploy. As flattering as all of this is to me, the story in Afghanistan has of course moved on, and with very tragic consequences – as the casualty rate in Afghanistan is now higher than that experienced at the height of Operation Telic in Iraq. 37 British troops were KIA during the 2009 summer Parliamentary recess alone.

I sadly anticipated that this would eventually be the case, and predicted it in my conclusion. Afghanistan today has effectively become the Devil's Playground, a place where conflict has no apparent end and where there are no visible signs of change to justify us pursuing the current strategy –it is not working, and is indeed tearing our NATO forces apart as they continually debate the best way forward.

For some military commanders, the situation has become intolerable as they feel they are fighting not just the Taliban, but their own political masters as well – as they plead their respective cases for more manpower and equipment to help in either the pacification or destruction of the enemy. Three years on, the Taliban now occupy more Afghan territory than they did in 2006, have more fighters – and more alarmingly – they seem to be gaining the upper hand in the psychological element of the conflict: the battle for the hearts and minds of the Afghan people. A key critical requirement.

There is also the matter of the equipment we field in Afghanistan. Have we got the right force balance, or is it overkill? Are we deploying unsuitable vehicles and weapons in our fight against the Taliban, or is it simply that the environment is just too demanding for them?

Perhaps we need to revisit previous conflicts and examine them like never before to see what lessons we could learn – and how they could be implemented in our Afghan master plan – to bring about a decisive outcome. Could it be that a previous strategy used elsewhere is our solution to this conflict? Sorting out Afghanistan's long list of issues – not to mention defeating the Taliban – is going to be a monumental task. Assuming that we can bring about such a miracle, will that be the end of the War on Terror? Sadly I fear not – as Yemen is already being viewed as Al-Qaeda's new Murder Inc HQ and no doubt, at some point in the future we are going to have to cross swords in this land also – whether we like it or not.

But before we get ahead of ourselves, we need to look at how the West and Pakistan are going to go about defeating Al-Qaeda's praetorian guard, the Taliban – the new masters of guerrilla warfare – who now reside in their own self-created Islamic Republic in Waziristan, Pakistan's own backyard. What do our Pakistani allies feel about this situation, and the long term implications for them? More importantly, what are they going to do about it? I hope there are some answers in *The Devil's Playground*.

Within NATO itself, the jury is well and truly out as to what is the best strategy to pursue in Afghanistan against the Taliban. However, the thoughts of each member of the ISAF Alliance are fairly academic: the US calls the shots in this war. But the Americans themselves are divided in their opinion as to what direction to take.

On one side is General Stanley McChrystal, Commander of International Forces in Afghanistan advocating a surge of 45,000 troops into the conflict as a means of dominating and shaping the ground in NATO's favour, a tactic previously used successfully in Iraq by General Petraeus as a means of suffocating the insurgency that was causing so much loss of life prior to its implementation.

On the other hand, in the White House there are those who want a more 'detached' conflict, with more use of unmanned aircraft and special forces and a vastly reduced direct role for ISAF. Meaning the Afghanistan National Army (ANA) would have to step up to the plate like never before. The man who has the unenviable job of ultimately deciding what strategy to follow is of course Barack Obama. And as if the military conundrum isn't already complicated enough, he also has to factor in the concerns raised by the fraudulent 2009 Afghan Presidential elections.

US soldier engaging Taliban in a fierce fire fight in Kunar province.

In November 2009, after what seemed like an eternity of vacillation, President Obama expressed his determination to 'finish the job' by sending more troops.

I

THE CRUCIBLE OF TERRORISM

British Prime Minister Gordon Brown described Afghanistan while on a visit there in April 2009, as 'a crucible for terrorism' responsible for fostering up to three-quarters of terror plots faced by the UK. It is a statistic that he and his Cabinet often repeat. This was his first return visit to Afghanistan following a decision to send more British troops into the country after the NATO summit held the previous month. His thoughts echoed those of Obama, who also viewed the Afghanistan–Pakistan border as central to future operations in the region.

There is however one key difference. Gordon Brown is pretty sold on the idea that the British are in this for the long haul, whereas President Obama – well, he's not so sure. The US Congress are starting to feel this. As one recently said ' George Bush fought the wrong war, whereas Barack Obama won't fight the right war.' He meant that Obama would not commit the requisite military resources and assets needed in Afghanistan to prevail. For America's staunchest ally – Britain – this is concerning as we are the second biggest military player in Afghanistan at this time. Why President Obama is holding back is obviously the subject of much conjecture. However one thing that we can be sure of is that his confidence in the Afghan government is absolutely at rock bottom – so things can only go up.

As for the British Prime Minister, Gordon Brown really has to fight the good fight, as the UK now has more Al-Qaeda activists and supporters living within the country than there are in the United States and indeed in the whole of Europe. The only way out is to defeat the Al-Qaeda ideology and everything it stands for. Britain is not alone in this situation either, as Pakistan has more Al-Qaeda and Taliban supporters living in and operating from its backyard than anyone. Hence the importance of Mr Brown's 2009 visit.

Meeting Pakistan's President Asif Ali Zardari he said 'There is a crucible of terrorism in the mountainous border between Afghanistan and Pakistan. Our approach to those countries is different but must be complementary.

Our strategy for dealing with this breeding ground of terrorism will mean more security on the streets of Britain.' He also told the Afghan president, Hamid Karzai while on the same tour: ' I come here as a friend of Afghanistan, wanting to continue to work with you in the best ways we can to strengthen the democracy of Afghanistan, to give support to the Afghan people, social, economic and political … help for the future and to join the work of eradicating terrorism from this area and, of course, from the borders of Pakistan as well.' His whirlwind tour was designed to reaffirm the UK's commitment to Afghanistan – following his announcement that an additional 900 extra troops along with £15m of aid was being provided as a means of supporting the 2009 Afghan elections. Had he known the disastrous outcome of these elections in advance, he may well have thought twice about this aid.

While on his visit he confirmed that the UK's £655m four-year aid package to Pakistan was being adjusted – with half of this vast sum being sent to support the country's troubled northern provinces – those areas often seen as the Taliban's main base of operations. He also expressed a desire to see more police being recruited in Afghanistan as their numbers are not enough to support the Afghan National Army, which itself is expanding from 75,000 to 134,000 personnel in the not too distant future. That makes it bigger than the British Army. Mr Brown continued:

> There is a chain of terrorism that goes from here round to the streets of Britain. That's why it's absolutely important that, while we have made progress on Afghan elections, democratic government, 6 million children in education, hospitals as well as roads and infrastructure for the people of Afghanistan, that we defeat international terrorism and hold it back from here in Lashkar Gar, here in Helmand province, but also on the other side of the border in Pakistan. I think it is right that we support an exercise by more than 40 countries who maintain democracy in Afghanistan against the Taliban and against the possibility of Al-Qaeda. I think it is very important that we work with the Pakistan government in countering terrorism.
>
> We know that three-quarters of the terrorist activities that happen in Britain arise from the areas around here. Therefore, the safety of people on the streets of Britain is immediately being safeguarded by the action being taken here.

This we should remember was one of the most important periods in Afghan history prior to their flawed elections – as all sides wanted to reaffirm their position, expectations and commitment to the country's future.

There were however a number of issues that needed ironing out, one of the most controversial arising out of the introduction of Sharia family law in Afghanistan – which would have legalised rape within marriage. President

USAF B1 on support mission over Afghanistan.
In August 2008 a B-1B flew the first Sniper
Advanced Targeting Pod (ATP)-equipped sortie
over Afghanstan, dropping a GBU-38 guided
bomb on enemy ground forces. The ATP is a
state-of-the-art laser long-range precision
targetting system.

Karzai, realising how sensitive this issue was, agreed to a review: 'I assure you that the law in Afghanistan will be completely in harmony with the constitution of Afghanistan and the human rights that we have (in our constitution) and with the principle of international treaties. I can tell you with confidence that the law is under review. Amendments will take place.' Ironically no sooner had he made this statement, it was discovered that there was another Afghan law that permitted the starvation of wives, if they refused their husbands sex. At this present time this law is also under review.

Gordon Brown at the start of his meeting with the Afghan president made a formal apology for the distress caused by civilian casualties. Speaking of this, he said 'Every life lost is a tragedy. Every civilian life lost is one too many. We are committed to avoiding civilian casualties by ensuring that our troops are trained and equipped.' He was of course referring to the unacceptable civilian casualties that had resulted from either poor targeting procedures or the over-reliance on air assets such as UAVs, perhaps over-used as a means of taking the fight to the Taliban, rather than engaging them with ground forces. Recently it was claimed in the United States that since 2006, only 14 mid level Al-Qaeda commanders have been killed by the many thousands of UAVs and armed drones that roam Afghanistan's skies every year – while at the same time they have allegedly killed according to Afghan sources some 700 civilians. That's a hit rate of 2 per cent on 98 per cent collateral. The US Department of Defense, however, utterly refutes these figures.

One thing nobody disputes is the fact that innocent civilians are being killed – and that must stop. In fairness to the British soldiers deployed in Helmand, they had at the time of Brown's speech already made a conscious effort to minimise their use of close air support – whereas with the US forces it was still very much a case of achieving objectives by overwhelming use of firepower. This of course at times led to a degree of resentment and frustration with the US policy, as British lives were being put on the line as a matter of routine so as to minimise Afghan casualties – whereas for Uncle Sam it was very much business as usual. The restraint of air power use by the British over a period of time led to Afghan confidence in them growing – as they could clearly see that they were deliberately putting their own soldiers' lives at greater risk.

Just as everyone felt that we were turning a corner in winning over the hearts and minds of the Afghan people, someone would drop a bomb carelessly, causing civilian casualties – and all that hard work would have been for nothing. The US have now accepted that much more effort must be put into avoiding civilian casualties – as every family that suffers a loss provides potential recruits for the Taliban. The Taliban are also exploiting Afghanistan's weak government and are making much mileage from the issue. Even President Karzai admitted that his government was weak:

The Afghan government does not have the abilities that other governments have. Had we been a fully capable state with the means and tools of governance in our hands, the troops of the rest of the world would not be here. You would not have given us the billions of dollars that you given us.

He is of course right about this, but the Afghan government really only have themselves to blame, as they have made little effort to sort out corruption and fraud within their ranks.

The greatest example of corruption currently being touted around Afghanistan at the time of writing (aside from those identified during the summer elections) concerns President Karzai's brother, Ahmed Wali Karzai, whose name has constantly been linked to drug trafficking. And yet the President and his western backers seemingly do nothing to address the problem. It would seem that part of the reason why a blind eye has been turned to some of his alleged activities is that Ahmed Karzai has been on the payroll of the CIA's SOG (Special Operations Group) for some eight years – giving him a lifetime get-out-of-jail card for services rendered. His role apparently has been to recruit a paramilitary force that operates in conjunction with the CIA in and around the Kandahar area. Known as the Kandahar Strike Force, this unit ironically operates out of the former home of the Taliban's founder, Mohammed Omar – which really must wind up the local branch of the Taliban. Maybe that's the idea! When a member of the CIA was asked recently to comment upon Ahmed Karzai's activities with them he said ' Virtually every significant Afghan figure has had brushes with the drug trade … If you are looking for Mother Teresa she doesn't live in Afghanistan.' Nor it seems does Mr Osama Bin Laden – Al Qaeda's leader.

Such situations of course illustrate just how complex and difficult everything is in Afghanistan in terms of getting anything done – there always seems to be a price for it one way or another. This of course does not make life easy for NATO and its soldiers as they go about their daily business of trying to bring stability to Afghanistan, often in the face of corruption that is beyond their control. NATO operates on a four-point doctrine that was launched in 2007 consisting of 'Afghan-isation', localisation, civilianisation, and reconciliation. All very interesting, but until the Taliban is defeated in Afghanistan, nothing major in the way of reconstruction, civilianisation or reconciliation is going to happen. Period. And the idea that we are going to see a democracy in Afghanistan that mirrors ours in the west any time soon is risible.

The buzz word at this present time in Afghanistan is reconstruction – via our PRTs (Provincial Reconstruction Teams). All very laudable, but how can our military support local civilians in their efforts to stop growing opium poppy when it pays so well compared to what we have to offer as an alternative? The reconstruction of Afghanistan is of course highly important – as the

West wants to show both the Afghans and indeed itself that tangible progress is being made. But in the current high threat environment that passes for daily life in Afghanistan this is extremely difficult. How can you possibly have workers trying to build new schools and hospitals when they are being either murdered or intimidated on a daily basis because there is no guaranteed regular protection for them – either from foreigners or their fellow countrymen in the Afghan Police and Army? Until there is, we cannot expect to see all Afghans displaying unflinching loyalty to the outsiders – and when deep down they are wondering how long will it be before they all walk – leaving them to a fate that doesn't really bear thinking about. This Afghan uncertainty has two main sources.

Firstly, there are a number of NATO members operating in Afghanistan at present that are seriously looking at withdrawing their forces from direct combat operations. They no longer wish their forces to be exposed to danger for a cause that, although not hopeless, seems to show no sign of improving in the short term. Secondly, there are simply not enough NATO boots on the ground to dominate and until there are, NATO cannot shape the battlefield that is Afghanistan in its favour. The Afghans see this all the time, when our forces are in their village one day promising them the earth, while the next day it's the Taliban giving them a gypsies' warning as to the consequences of cooperating with the infidel. Indeed compared to 2002, they now hold less ground than the Taliban, who have more influence over the Afghan people in certain areas – and NATO is taking far more casualties than it did back then. So what has gone wrong?

In my opinion NATO took its eyes off the ball in Afghanistan after 2002, and it is only recently that it has started to focus again on what needs to be done to defeat the Taliban once and for all. The people of Afghanistan only understand what they see, and not what is said.

A British Jackal waves the flag during Op Aabi Toorah.

Afghan locals help a British Warrior crew change a damaged track during Op Panther's Claw. Many felt obliged to help the British troops, as they were after all laying their lives on the line in order to enable the Afghan elections.

Wounded Afghan civilians stagger away after being hit by a NATO air strike. Such terrible scenes only serve as a recruiting sergeant for the Taliban. Avoiding such terrible 'collateral damage' is paramount.

Afghanistan's President Karzai.

WILD FRONTIERS

It is my belief that Afghanistan's long term peace and prosperity prospects could be substantially improved if the Taliban could be denied permanently the ability to recruit, train and operate freely from their neighbour, Pakistan. In very recent history, such an outcome would have seemed unlikely as Pakistan – the creators of the Taliban – had a vested interest in supporting them. Instability in Afghanistan was clearly seen as being good for Pakistan.

Today however there has been a seismic shift in the attitude of the Pakistani government as they are just as likely to be victims of the Taliban as their Afghan neighbours. Essentially, if you keep wild dogs in your back-yard sooner or later they are going to turn on you. And that is exactly what has happened in Pakistan.

Some elements of the Pakistani Armed Forces (PAF) and the ISI operated a relatively open border policy, which allowed the Taliban to go into Afghanistan and carry out hit and run operations against British soldiers in Helmand – the mindset of these misguided individuals being that, if the Taliban had free movement from one area to another they were going to be far less likely to turn on the people offering them a safe haven. How wrong they were. This situation caused immense frustration in the West, and led to pressure being put on Pakistan's then President, General Pervez Musharaff, to close the border and then take effective action against the Taliban who were hiding out in Waziristan.

At first his actions were relatively limited and weak as he was obviously mindful of the upset that he was going to cause within his own country once he commenced any form of serious military intervention that went beyond that of a local internal policing action. Also in the back of his mind was the fact that if he pushed the Taliban too hard there was a very high probability that elements within his own secret service, the ISI, would turn on him. He was damned either way.

Pakistan has nuclear weapons – and it is in nobody's interest for them to fall into the hands of the Taliban. This single fact was Musharaff's ace as he could use it both as a bargaining chip to gain more financial and military aid from the West, and at the same time he would be seen by the vast majority of his own people as being their protector from the ultimate nightmare. Mr Musharaff would have made a great poker player it would seem. But this was no game, and he knew it.

Prior to the application of US political pressure, what is often not appreciated by most people in the West is the fact that Pakistani forces had on a number of previous occasions over the years already engaged both Al-Qaeda and the Taliban during combat operations around their border area. The first of these actually occurred in 2002, when Pakistani troops entered both North and South Waziristan, their first military incursion into the region since Pakistan's independence in 1947. The purpose was to persuade the Waziri tribes to hand over any Al-Qaeda militants hiding amongst them; but fearing that they were being subjugated, in 2004 the rebel tribesmen began an undeclared war with the Pakistani military that lasted for almost two years. During the intense fighting that took place, two assassination attempts were made against President Musharraf – both sanctioned from Waziristan. These personal attacks caused a massive increase in Pakistani military activity against both the Waziri tribes and their AQT (Al-Qaeda/Taliban) friends who were now living amongst them. It should be borne in mind that Waziristan has always seen itself as being independent and Pakistani military incursion in Waziri territory was always going to be resented.

Initially, in 2002, the Waziri tribes were surprisingly tolerant of the Pakistani military presence, partly because it had been negotiated and also because there was the promise of aid and money. But like many things in Afghanistan and Pakistan, there is always a fear that other agendas are being pursued. Not helping matters is the geography of Waziristan itself, which lends itself perfectly to guerrilla warfare. This aspect of the terrain has been exploited for centuries. There is an abundance of places to hide out in. No doubt Bin Laden knows a fair few of them!

The PAF (Pakistan Armed Forces) have had a rough time there, having fought and then negotiated a number of peace deals with the Taliban – only to see them broken time after time following an incident elsewhere that has negated them. It must be stressed that these peace deals are only negotiated for Pakistan's benefit and certainly not for Afghanistan's, a thorny issue. They are also extremely complicated. For example, in June 2006, the military head of the Taliban in Waziristan, Sirajuddin Haqqani, issued a decree that there were to be no more attacks on the Pakistani Army, this was to be the new Taliban policy. This indeed calmed things down in south Waziristan but not in north Waziristan where it was business as usual because the decree was never circulated there. This tactic was quite deliberate by the Taliban, as they wanted to show the Pakistanis just how much power and control they had in the region. This gave them much more bargaining power later, when negotiating a comprehensive accord more to their advantage.

On September 5 2006, the Waziristan Accord, an agreement between the Pakistani government and local tribal leaders, was signed in Miranshah, North Waziristan, to end all fighting. The agreement contained the following provisions:

1. The Pakistani Army will help reconstruct infrastructure in tribal areas of North and South Waziristan.
2. The Pakistani Military will not tolerate any assistance to intruders in North Waziristan, and will monitor actions in the region.
3. The Pakistan government is to compensate tribal leaders for the loss of life and property of innocent tribesmen.
4. 'Foreigners '(informally understood to be foreign jihadists) are not allowed to use Pakistani territory for any terrorist activity anywhere in the world.
5. 2,500 foreigners who were originally held on suspicion of having links to the Taliban are to be detained for necessary action against them.

This agreement was seen as something of a coup for the Pakistani government – and a positive move towards a permanent peace – but that was not be. Barely had the ink dried, and it was business as usual after two major incidents. The first came on October 30 2006, when the PAF carried out an air strike against a madrassa in the Bajour region on the Afghan border, killing some 80 people. This was quickly followed by a retaliation suicide bombing against an army camp on November 8 2006, which killed 42 Pakistani soldiers and wounded another 20.

Following these two events there was a whole series of internal tribal feuds and AQT attacks that involved more blood being shed across the various regions – far too many to cover here. (These numerous events were nothing to what was to follow. For reasons of brevity, I am only listing the key events and battles.)

Lal Masjid Siege and War in Waziristan

On July 3 2007, there was a clash in Islamabad between Pakistani security forces and students from the Lal Masjid mosque after they attacked a government building with stones. What then followed was a stand-off which gradually escalated to a siege of the mosque – despite the intervention of the Pakistan

Above: Pakistani forces on patrol in southern Waziristan.

Left: Smoke rises in Peshawar after an attack against Taliban militants in the city.

Muslim League. On July 11 the siege ended with the loss of 108 lives. This siege effectively brought an end to the Waziristan Peace Accord and was the catalyst for worse to come. Shortly after the Lal Masjid mosque incident, there followed a series of tit-for-tat attacks on Pakistani soldiers and security forces, mainly suicide bombings, killing 69 personnel and wounding more than 100.

In response, the army moved back into Waziristan en masse and engaged in fierce clashes with the Taliban and other militants, costing the dissidents some 100 fatalities, including wanted terrorist Abdullah Mehsud, a former Guantanamo Bay detainee. The militants of course struck back at Pakistani military convoys and check points, killing dozens of soldiers, police and civilians. In one month of serious fighting from July 24 to August 24 2007, some 250 militants and 60 soldiers were killed.

On September 2 2007, the militants carried out a spectacular ambush on a 17-vehicle Pakistani Army convoy – capturing 247 soldiers – without firing a single shot. You would have thought at this point that the PAF would have upped their game; instead they suffered even more losses after the Taliban hit them with multiple attacks up and down both northern and southern Waziristan.

These attacks were primarily on remote outposts and checkpoints, seen as soft targets. Five were completely overrun, resulting in some 65 soldiers either killed or captured along with almost 100 wounded. For the Pakistani Army this was the final straw, and they retaliated with helicopter gunships, close air support aircraft, artillery and substantial ground forces. The main focus of their attack was the town of Mir Ali. Over a period of four days from October 7 to October 10 2007 they killed 175 Taliban, for the loss of 47 soldiers.

The Swat Valley Offensive

Following this operation, the focus of attention switched to the Swat district of North-West Frontier Province, after a large force of Taliban tried to impose strict Islamic Sharia Law upon a number of towns and villages in the Swat valley. This particular event sent shock waves through the Pakistani government, as this area had always been deemed peaceful by Pakistani standards – it even had a ski resort. To counter this threat the Pakistani Government sent in 3,000 paramilitaries, some of whom performed really well against the Taliban, while others proved not to be up to the task. About 220 of them along with some local police either surrendered or deserted after their hill top positions were attacked and overrun. Their failure left the Swat valley almost completely under Taliban control.

Their dominance did not last for long as in November 2007, 2,500 regular Pakistani troops supported by helicopter gunships were sent in. By early December they had prevailed, leaving some 400 Taliban and their supporters dead for the loss of 15 of their own number. This was not the end of the matter as in 2008 new Taliban forces began creeping back into the area until they eventually occupied and controlled almost 80 per cent of the valley – despite numerous battles to stop them.

Eventually, in January 2009, the Pakistani government controversially agreed to the imposition of Sharia law in the area and the suspension of further military operations, to the outrage of the US government who saw this move as one that would further strengthen the Taliban's grip on their country. The US pointed out that in addition to Waziristan the Taliban would now have a second major sanctuary in which to hide and train – only 80 miles from Pakistan's capital, Islamabad. As the months went by, the Taliban drifted back to their old habits – including publicly whipping a 17-year-old girl after she refused a marriage proposal. Unluckily for them it was caught on video and broadcast across Pakistan, causing an outcry. Protests broke out everywhere demanding an end to the barbaric practice, which showed the world that the vast majority of Pakistanis wanted nothing to do with the practices of these bigoted thugs.

Among those who spoke out was Raja Zafar ul-Haq, a well known and highly respected Pakistani Islamic scholar who stated that the flogging was totally un-Islamic and had nothing to do with Sharia law. He then went on to say that the Prophet Muhammad had strictly forbidden the practice of forced marriage, and in his view by definition the girl had every right to refuse the proposal. The Pakistani government, taken aback by the public outpouring, decided that they needed to be seen to do something about the situation in the Swat valley once and for all. They ordered their troops back into the Swat in Operation Black Thunderstorm.

Operation Black Thunderstorm

The second Swat offensive commenced on April 26 2009, and involved a major operation to push the Taliban out of Buner, Lower Dir, Swat and Shangla districts – all areas that had seen intense conflict with the Taliban at some time or other. The operation cleared the Taliban out of a number of these areas relatively quickly, but the battle for the Swat valley was particularly intense and vicious on account of the Taliban engaging the Pakistani Army head to head in pitched battles, rather than in their normal asymmetric manner. The offensive eventually reached its climax on May 23 when a major battle took place for the city of Mingora – an action which lasted for five days.

This battle effectively ended the Taliban's grip on the Swat valley, although mopping up operations continued for several months. Casualties on both sides were high, with 1,475 Taliban confirmed dead – 23 of whom were foreigners. The Pakistani Army reported 128 killed and 317 wounded. In addition, 95 soldiers and police were captured by the Taliban. Eighteen escaped – the fate of the rest is unknown. The Pakistani Army also captured 114 Taliban, a number of whom were local commanders.

Other significant operations around this time included the defeat of the Taliban and other extremists in the battle for the Bajaur region, which lies on the Afghan border. This offensive lasted for six months and left some 1,500 Taliban dead, while Pakistani Army losses were put at 97 soldiers killed and 404 wounded.

The Blockade of South Waziristan

Also around the same time as the battle for Bajaur was taking place, another major offensive was launched against south Waziristan – the mission being to eliminate the Taliban's leader in Pakistan, Baitullah Mehsud, along with his estimated 20,000 men. Mehsud was once described as 'the root of all evils' and his demise was a top priority. The US at the time of the offensive launch were full of praise for the Pakistani government as they now felt that they were at last taking appropriate action. The Pakistanis of course had gone after Mehsud on a number of occasions before in 2004, 2005, 2008 and now 2009, but just as they were finally closing in on him a US UAV got there first with a precision strike. As everyone was celebrating his demise, another Taliban extremist, Hakimullah Mehsud, slid into his shoes. Incensed by the death of Mehsud, the Taliban embarked on a major series of attacks both inside Afghanistan and Pakistan, to make sure everyone got the message that they were still very much alive and killing.

The first of these attacks occurred on October 5. Five UN workers were killed when a suicide bomber dressed up as a police officer blew himself up in the World Food Program office in Islamabad. Then on October 9, a suicide bomber killed 53 civilians and wounded over 100 in a Bazaar in Peshawar. On October 10, ten Taliban commandos dressed in Pakistani military uniforms attacked the General Headquarters in Rawalpindi, taking a number of hostages. After 22 hours the siege ended following a special forces assault in which the Taliban's leader was taken alive. This incident cost 23 lives: 12 soldiers, nine Taliban and two civilians. Amongst the dead were a brigadier and a lieutenant colonel.

October 12, and a suicide bomber kills 45 people, including six soldiers in a market in Shangla. October 15, and the Taliban carry out five coordinated assaults on police forces in three cities – leaving 41 people dead, including 10 Taliban. Amongst the dead is an eight-year old child. October 21, five civilians are killed and 22 wounded following two suicide bomb attacks on an Islamic University. October 28, and Pakistan suffers its worst attack on civilians yet; 91 are killed and over 200 wounded by a car bomb in a busy market in Peshawar. Most of the dead are women and children leaving a mosque. This probably ranks as one of the most cowardly and despicable attacks ever perpetrated by the Taliban.

Pakistani Politics

Even without the Taliban, life for a Pakistani politician is always fraught – you never know when you are going to appear on an assassin's list. In this present climate of constant Taliban attacks how long is it before Pakistan declares a state of emergency as it did in 2007? That November, the last emergency was declared by President Pervez Musharraf, during which the constitution of the country was suspended for a month purportedly because of the actions of Islamic militants in Waziristan. There was always a sneaking suspicion that it was a ploy to get Mr Musharraf re-elected without having to go through the tiresome democratic process.

Whether that is true or not, what is not in doubt is that Pakistan today has some serious internal as well as external issues to deal with. I can remember in particular my thoughts before the assassination of Pakistani opposition leader Benazir Bhutto on December 27 2007 in Rawalpindi, Pakistan. I felt that it was only a matter of time before this brave woman became another victim to be added to the long list of those who have tried to heal Pakistan. Of course as soon as she died the blame game started, with President Musharraf blaming Al-Qaeda, while Taliban commander Baitullah Mehsud blamed him. Hundreds lost their lives as a consequence.

Pakistani politics is a mystery to the westerner looking in, as is the complex Waziristan situation – which receives relatively little western media coverage. In fact, at the time of writing there is not a single western journalist there. Perhaps this is because the CIA deems Waziristan the most dangerous place on earth. What does come out through official Pakistani sources tends to be biased, giving little away about how big the problem is or how well its armed forces are dealing with it. Certainly, we see plenty of coverage from Pakistan itself – after a bomb explodes or there is some form of attack – but only because we have so many reporters based there. What is missing is the story behind the story. Today Waziristan is effectively an Islamic Republic run by the Taliban with the support of Al-Qaeda. How has the 'Talibanization'of this region been allowed to happen right under everyone's noses – without being checked?

This nightmare situation for Pakistan has occurred because prior to the last three years its military intervention in Waziristan has been patchy and lacking real commitment. It is only now, after Pakistan has been the victim of so many multiple armed attacks and bombings that it has decided to go on an all-out military offensive against the Taliban and its numerous supporters living in its own back-yard. Maybe they could learn some lessons from the Soviets who were also the victims of attacks from Waziristan.

Pakistani soldiers prepare for a Taliban attack during Operation Bara.

Executed by the Taliban.

Pakistani forces in a dominant hilltop position in southern Waziristan take stock after days of intense fighting.

An illustration of how Taliban justice is typically applied.

LEARNING FROM THE BEARS

It would be very easy for any armchair general to form the conclusion that the Russians lost their war in Afghanistan, so therefore there is nothing to be learned from them. They would be wrong as there is something to be learned from the tactics they employed against the Mujahideen – and how and why they failed to win over the Afghan people. The latter comes as little surprise as they made almost no effort to engage with them, except through the barrel of a gun.

In my previous book *Battlefield Afghanistan*, I covered Soviet military tactics employed in Afghanistan compared to ours and this part of the book is often given to soldiers about to go to Afghanistan as a tactical guide. It is my aim here to cover not so much what they did wrong, but what they did right. If we look at their performance at the tactical level, they only ever won actions when they had local command autonomy. When they reverted to operational command their success rate dropped. At local level, their officers had good knowledge of the terrain where they were based and what threat level they were likely to face. This meant that they could shape their forces in response far more effectively. They also found that by gaining local terrain knowledge, they could defeat the Mujahideen at their own game as they would be able to anticipate ambush points, block likely escape routes and ultimately deny the enemy any form of local psychological advantage.

One key difference between then and now is that the western forces respect the local Afghan population and do everything possible to avoid them becoming victims of collateral damage, whereas with the Russians no such sentiments were shown. They would openly exploit the local Afghans. For instance they dropped small mines from the air that looked like butterflies, which they intended should be picked up by young children and taken back to their villages, causing casualties. It might come as something of a surprise that there were times when the Mujahideen came perilously close to being defeated – simply through the unrelenting brutality inflicted upon them and their families.

The tide only really turned in the Mujahideen's favour when the West began supplying indirect military assistance to them along with two lethal weapon systems – MANPADs (Man-Portable Air Defence Systems) and anti-tank missiles. Without them the outcome for the Soviets may have been different. Although NATO does not yet face a significant MANPAD threat from the Taliban, it may well yet come – as discussed in the next chapter. And although our forces do not face the threat of anti-tank missiles, they do face the IED – currently the Taliban's weapon of choice.

Speaking of weapons, one topic that is currently a major source of heated debate amongst NATO members in Afghanistan is personnel weapons and the calibre of round that they are using. The standard size of round used against the Taliban is the NATO 5.56mm, which in close-quarter combat is fine, but for long range engagements it just does not have enough stopping power at 600m plus. This lack of punch has forced our soldiers at section and platoon level to revert to carrying belt fed 7.62 machine guns such as the GPMG (General Purpose Machine Gun), which is able to lay down accurate fire up to 1,800m, and 3000m if used in the sustained fire role, which requires the use of a tripod. The Taliban are not great fans of this type of weapon, nor indeed do they like the .50 cal heavy machine gun, which has even greater range and stopping power. As one soldier recently said ' 5.56 mm the Taliban ignore; 7.62mm worries them; .50 calibre scares them.'

Engagements in Afghanistan tend to take place between 500m and 900m making it extremely difficult for our soldiers to locate, suppress and kill their enemy. The Taliban understandably do not make themselves easy targets and are very skilful at making good use of cover. It is not unusual for NATO soldiers to admit that during firefights they seldom if ever actually see their enemy. This gives some indication of the distances that are involved in such actions.

One area where the West certainly has learned from the Russian experience is in the use of snipers. At one point this skill was almost extinct in the British Army, but these days it is very much alive, with record numbers of personnel now trained to take on this demanding role. Currently the weapon of choice for British snipers is the Accuracy International 7.62mm L96. However, higher calibres such as .50 are also available for longer range requirements – these usually in the hands of special forces.

The Russians in Afghanistan made extensive use of helicopters in their operations, which the British also do – when they have them! Helicopters are a touchy subject for the British forces deployed in Afghanistan. Despite more having been sent out they still have nowhere near enough, and frequently have to call upon their US allies for the loan of theirs.

The Russians had great success against the Mujahideen – prior to the introduction of Stingers – employing close air support. Unlike modern, relatively delicate aircraft, Russian aircraft used in Afghanistan were far more rugged.

Clockwise from left:
An 82nd Airborne machine gunner trains his lethal .50 HMG at a possible target.

The USAF A10 Thunderbolt 11, probably the finest CAS aircraft in service in Afghanistan today. Its 30mm Gatling gun is greatly feared by the Taliban. It sounds like a buzz saw.

Australian recce vehicles from the special operations task group – as seen through the marvels of night vision.

This image of a US soldier climbing a rocky escarpment gives a pretty good idea of how tough and demanding the terrain is in Afghanistan.

They inspired the design of the US A-10 Warthog. Until Stinger arrived they pretty much enjoyed open season against the Mujahideen, and often inflicted immense losses upon them, of both life and materiel. The Russians were extremely good at orchestrating attacks that involved both ground and air assets, using a tactic called Hammer and Anvil. NATO now use a very similar tactic in Afghanistan inspired by their hard-learned combat lessons.

The Russians employed the highly lethal Mil-24 Hind helicopter gunship to good effect. This helicopter at the time of its deployment was years ahead of its time, and caused great alarm in the West – basically they had nothing to match it. This is partly why they supported Russia's enemies with such commitment. Afghanistan was the perfect testing ground for new weapons. Until Stinger arrived, the Mujahideen had always referred to the Hind as the Devil's Chariot, as up until that point they had virtually nothing in their armoury that would bring it down. All that of course changed once Uncle Sam got involved in their 'dirty war'.

Lessons Learned

There is no doubt that the West learned a vast amount from the Soviet experience in Afghanistan about how its weapons systems performed against the mighty Russian war machine – albeit through surrogate users. Yet, at the most basic tactical level, NATO seems almost always to ignore the lessons learned from the Mujahideen success. This is extremely foolish. If those lessons were applied casualties would be reduced and western forces would be more combat effective.

UK forces have upped their game since 2006 and are now arguably amongst the best trained soldiers in the world for this deployment. To illustrate this point, early in 2009 the UK opened a purpose built training centre in Norfolk, which features both a realistic Afghan village and a compound typical of those found in the rural areas of the country. The Afghan 'village', named Sindh Kalay, even comes complete with a market run by Dari-speaking retired Gurkhas, whose presence helps create a truly realistic Afghan scene. Such training is vital to soldiers undergoing their OPTAG work-up phase and no doubt greatly helps them in their deployment preparation.

It is anticipated that some 80,000 personnel will be put through this training village annually, including other NATO members who wish to better prepare their soldiers for what lies ahead of them. Cross training with other NATO members is also good for soldiers as they learn to appreciate each other's combat skills as well as the weapons and equipment they respectively employ. In a number of operations, particularly around the time of the Afghan elections, British and ANA soldiers were in action together supported by Danish Leopard tanks, Australian gunners as well as US air assets operated under British control. So interoperability is clearly evident.

Mujahideen IEDs

Despite what has been written in the past about the Mujahideen not using IEDs against the Soviets, I can categorically confirm that they did use them. Their favourite one was the linked shell IED, as the Mujahideen had easy access to them, either by way of looting Russian convoys or by raids on Afghan-held armouries. For this IED to be effective all they had to do was link two or three shells together under a road which were then connected to either a command wire or mine – and there you have it, one instant IED. easily capable of destroying a BTR APC or light tank.

Other favourites included sending donkeys and horses over heavily guarded wooden bridges while petrol leaked from special saddles that were attached to them – the puddles of fuel later being ignited by snipers firing tracer rounds. Simple but very effective. And finally, one that the Mujahideen had great success with, as do the Taliban today: the Chinese ice rocket. A rocket such as a Chinese 107mm is planted in a tube buried amongst either rocks or mud, pointing in the general direction of a large fixed target such as an airfield. Once set up they wait until the coldest part of the night, and then plant a block of ice between the bottom of the rocket and its igniter. Then as dawn breaks, and the sun gets warmer the ice melts, the rocket slides down the tube hitting the igniter and fires. The setters are of course by then long gone. Only by dominating the ground in strength can you prevent such attacks, as the Russians found out the hard way. It would seem, we still have a lot to learn from their experience.

A British BDO hard at work clearing Kabul airport of its lethal Soviet legacies.

Royal Marine sniper team.

Royal Marines take 5. Notice the wide variety of weaponry that they have to carry during routine patrols.

Above left A Royal Marine with an SA80 A2 grenade launcher scopes out a possible target.

Above British .50 cal HMG gunner maintaining force protection.

Left Welsh Guards engaging the Taliban following an ambush. Note the nearest soldier's heavily modified SA 80A2 5.56mm assault rifle.

Left to right: US Special Forces soldier c. 2002.

Taliban fighter with RPG.

A sniper keeps watch.

IV

DODGING THE GOLDEN BB

During the Second World War US bomber crews flying high over Germany often referred to 'dodging the Golden BB', it being the one lucky shot that hits a vital component of an aircraft and brings it down. For the vast majority of aircrew operating high above the mountains and desert regions of Afghanistan, there is little chance of them being shot down by a Golden BB as the Taliban possess little in the way of effective anti-aircraft artillery. However, the same cannot be said for the helicopter aircrew operating at low level as they face an extremely high threat factor – generally from machine guns and RPGs, and on the odd occasion even truck-mounted cannons. Their most vulnerable time is during the insertion and extraction phase of a mission, as the Taliban know exactly where they are. But it is not just the Taliban that they have to be wary of.

On September 25 2008, Pakistani forces tried to shoot down two US military helicopters that were flying near their border. The Pakistanis alleged that the Americans had actually over-flown their territory, which according to them, gave the right to engage. Speaking later of this incident, Pakistan's President Zardari said ' Just as we will not let Pakistan's territory be used by terrorists for attacks against our people and our neighbours, we cannot allow our territory and our sovereignty to be violated by our friends.' With friends like that…

It is no secret that the biggest fear in Afghanistan is of the loss of a fully loaded Chinook. The consequences of that really don't bear thinking about. In addition to small arms fire, machine guns and RPGs the other threat is MANPADS such as the Stinger and SA-7 Grail. It is known that both Al-Qaeda and the Taliban have access to a number of different types but as yet to the best of my knowledge they have not used them. This may be down to a lack of training or serviceability problems. But they do have them. This was confirmed when US intelligence found components of SA-14 Gremlins in western Afghanistan in early 2009.

This particular weapon is highly effective and was used to shoot down a British Army Lynx helicopter over Basra in May 2006, killing all five on board.

It is also known that some US Stingers are still in circulation – a legacy of the Russian invasion – the type having being used against them by their western backed enemies the Mujahideen. It is no secret that these weapons decimated both the Russian ground attack and helicopter fleets to such a degree that they could not operate over Afghanistan without a high level of risk. They played a significant part in bringing about the Soviet defeat.

Stingers are highly effective weapons, however they are dependent on a battery power source to make them operable, and it is believed that any Stinger left over from the Russian period of occupation would now be ineffective. The same cannot be said for more recently acquired MANPADS supplied both directly and indirectly from Eritrea, Iran, Pakistan, Somalia and Syria, as these would only be a few years old. During one raid in Afghanistan, Commander of Afghan State military units in Kandahar, General Sher Muhammad Zazi confirmed that his forces had found large amounts of Iranian-supplied weapons – which surprises most observers as the Iranians are not great fans of the Taliban, yet they are supplying them.

When operating over Afghanistan, all NATO helicopters and aircraft assume that there will be a direct threat to them and employ counter-measures as a matter of routine. Although these are highly effective generally, some MANPADS such as the Russian SA-14 Gremlin and Chinese HN-5 are particularly difficult to throw off once locked on. For obvious reasons I am not going to outline specific areas of vulnerability with these systems. Current intelligence assessments indicate that the Taliban may be planning a spectacular – a mass use of MANPADS in one operation – but as yet no specific threat has been identified. As a means of recovering MANPADS in rogue circulation, US intelligence officers and agents are offering rewards for their recovery, a tactic used very successfully in Iraq, where they have recovered 121 since 2006 alone. This practice of buy-back is not new, as the CIA spent millions of dollars – as part of Operation Cyclone – to recover Stingers not used during the Soviet occupation of Afghanistan. The number of MANPADS available is currently estimated to be in excess of 1,500.

As well as AAA and MANPADS, aircrew also face serious danger from brownouts – when sand and dust gets kicked up by the rotor blades of a helicopter during either its landing or take-off causing reduced visibility and disorientation for the aircrew. The following is a breakdown of Chinook losses and their respective causes since ground operations commenced in 2001. To date, 15 Chinooks have been lost in Afghanistan as a result of either ground fire or heavy landings.

In January 2002 a US Army CH-47D assigned to A Company, 7th Battalion, 101st Airborne Division was destroyed following an extremely heavy landing brought about by brownout conditions, resulting in 16 of the 24 personnel on board being injured. In March 2002 two US Chinooks were lost during

Clockwise from top left: A packed Chinook in flight. The consequences of losing one like this in action do not bear thinking about.

CH53E Super Stallion over Bastion – one of only a handful of NATO helicopters capable of operating efficiently in Afghanistan's hot and high environment.

An RAF Chinook flares on approach to Laskar Ghar.

US ground crew hard at work preparing a Chinook for another mission over hell.

A Chinook loadmaster watching the Afghan world whizzing by beneath him.

Operation Anaconda – both brought down by ground fire around the Takur Ghar ridge – resulting in the deaths of six US Service personnel. April 2005, and a US CH-47 is lost to a brownout, causing the loss of 18 on board. June 2005, and 16 more personnel are killed following the loss of a US Chinook to an RPG. September 2005, and another US Chinook is lost in the eastern province of Zabul, five crew killed. Also in 2005, two Royal Netherlands Air Force (RNLAF) CH-47Ds were abandoned and later destroyed following heavy landings that damaged them beyond viable repair. No casualties resulted from either incident. In 2006, another US CH-47 is shot down, resulting in the loss of ten service personnel. February 2007, and a US Special Forces MH-47 is lost in Zabul province killing eight of the fourteen on board. May 2007, and all seven on board a US Chinook are killed following a crash during an operation. January 2009, and one US soldier is killed following a Chinook crash in eastern Afghanistan. August 19 2009, and a UK RAF HC2 Chinook is lost to heavy ground fire following a supply mission in Sangin. It transpired that the helicopter had taken multiple hits around its engine area, resulting in a fire that forced an emergency landing. Fortunately, all on board survived and were quickly rescued by another RAF Chinook flying close by. The grounded helicopter was then destroyed to deny the Taliban access to any weaponry or sensitive equipment carried, a common practice if recovery is impossible owing to difficult location or strong enemy presence.

Later in the same month, another RAF Chinook was lost following a heavy landing which damaged the undercarriage, nose and front blades of the helicopter so badly that it could not be flown out for repair. As in the previous incident the helicopter was destroyed, but this time by means of explosives rather than an air strike. All four aircrew were immediately extracted by another Chinook engaged on the same operation, while its fourteen passengers, all members of The Rifles Battlegroup, continued with their mission. Commenting on the loss of the first RAF Chinook, Lt Col Nick Richardson said: 'It is a measure of the bravery and skill of the pilots that operating under enemy fire, they were able to complete their task and calmly move to safety. Their cool under pressure has ensured that their lives were saved and minimal damage was caused despite the loss of one aircraft. The brave crew have thwarted insurgents' attempts to destabilise the elections with a shocking spectacular loss of British life.'

British Chinooks receiving ground fire is of course nothing new in Afghanistan, many have been hit, but through the skill and courage of their pilots they have managed to limp back to base for repair. One pilot lost two Chinooks to ground fire in one day – but still went out again in another to help rescue injured soldiers who were in urgent need of medical treatment.

October 2009 was a particularly bad month for helicopter losses with four incidents reported – all US Forces. The worst of these involved the loss of a

US MH-47G which crashed in western Afghanistan on October 26 killing seven US service personnel and three DEA (Drug Enforcement Agency) agents. 26 other passengers on board were also injured. There have been many other helicopter and aircraft losses in Afghanistan and these are listed below.

Rotary-Wing Losses

Type	Number Lost	Hostile Fire
AB-212	1	
AH-1 Supercobra	1	
AH-64 Apache	9	
UH-60 Blackhawk	9	2
CH-47 Chinook	20	6
CH-53E Super Stallion	1	
CH-53G Sea Stallion	2	
CH-146 Griffon	1	
Cougar AS532	2	
HH-60 Pave Hawk	3	
MH-53 Pave Low	2	
MH-6J	1	
Mil Mi-17	2	
Mil Mi-24	1	1
OH-58 Kiowa	2	1
UH-1N Huey	2	
Total	59 (10 to hostile fire)	

Fixed-Wing Losses

Type	Number Lost	Hostile Fire
F-15 Eagle	1	
F-16 Falcon	2	
C-130 Hercules	4	
GR-4 Tornado	1	
MC-130 Talon/Shadow	2	
Nimrod MR2	1	
P-3 Orion	1	
U-2	1	
B-1 Lancer	1	
Harrier	2	1
Total	16 (1 to hostile fire while on ground)	

Brownouts

At the time of writing, much effort is being expended in finding a permanent solution to the problem of brownouts. Contrary to popular belief, wearing night vision goggles does not solve it, as NVGs only amplify existing light. A weird phenomenon seen in both Iraq and Afghanistan is where sparks appear to be flying off the rotor blades as dust hits them – an effect called 'Pixie Dust.' There is however one helicopter that seems to cope with brownouts incredibly well and that is the British Merlin, currently scheduled for deployment to Afghanistan in early 2010 once its crews have completed their work-up training in El Cino, California. The location offers hot and high conditions not too dissimilar to those experienced in Afghanistan.

Why the Merlin should perform better than any other comparable helicopter in brownouts is uncertain. However it is believed that the wing-tips on the end of the Merlin's blades – known as BERPs – help create a 'doughnut' effect around the helicopter, which allows the aircrew just about enough visibility in dusty conditions to land and take-off safely. Brownout is a serious problem that needs addressing as a matter of urgency; three out of every four helicopter losses sustained in Afghanistan and Iraq are currently attributed to it. Maybe the Brits have the answer already.

Above: The shell of another lost Chinook is recovered.

Above right: An RAF Harrier GR9 over Afghanistan.

Right: An RAF Merlin FROM 78 Squadron flares for a landing in Helmand shortly after being deployed to the region. This particular type of helicopter is one of the best in ISAF service for coping with brownout conditions.

Chinooks making a low level pass to avoid possible MANPAD threats.

US Sea Knights flare for a landing following a major operation in southern Afghanistan.

V

BULLET MAGNETS

In my last book about Afghanistan I took just about every opportunity possible to make my views known about the lack of suitable armoured vehicles and equipment available to British soldiers – and in the process stirred up quite a hornet's nest. I was not alone in my thoughts, as many politicians, senior military commanders and the good old British press also campaigned for better kit. Three years on, what a difference.

Although not completely where they need to be, the UK Ministry of Defence (MoD) have to their credit done a great job in transforming fighting capability at the sharp end; their soldiers' individual equipment levels are now amongst the best in the world – if not *the* best in certain areas. One other area where they have really made dramatic improvements is that of vehicle protection. Back in 2006, British soldiers had little choice when it came to military vehicles. Today there are several new types that have either entered service in Afghanistan or are about to. British commanders on the ground can now quite literally choose which type of vehicle is best suited to their mission profile, a situation that would have been quite unimaginable a few years ago.

If protecting a convoy they can opt for a Mastiff, Vector, Viking or a Ridgeback. Or if on a long range recce or fighting patrol they can deploy the Jackal, an all-terrain vehicle that is very popular with the troops on account of its excellent off-road performance and lethal firepower. The MoD has spent over a billion pounds just on new types of vehicles – and these acquisitions are by no means over. When bringing into service new types of kit and vehicles quickly there is always going to be a need for further refinement or in some cases complete withdrawal when the new equipment has not performed as expected. A good example is the six-wheeled Vector, a vehicle designed to both replace and complement the infamous 'Snatch' Landrover – a vehicle loathed by all who have to risk driving in it, as it provides almost zero protection from IEDs, the scourge of Afghanistan.

In the case of the Vector, as one Army officer commented: 'It has just enough protection to lull you into a false sense of security, and it's only when you go over a mine you realise that it does not do what it says on the tin.' At one stage things got so bad that soldiers refused to sit over the axles, as they knew a mine or IED detonating underneath these points would be bad news for all concerned. At the time of writing, it is currently being withdrawn from service in Afghanistan, as confidence in its protection levels and reliability has plummeted. In some cases it is being replaced by the Vixen – an up-armoured version of the 'Snatch', which is ironic.

The contrast between the Vector and the British Army's current favourite vehicle, the Mastiff – a variant of the US Cougar – could not be greater. Almost all soldiers given a choice opt for it and no soldier at the time of writing has either been killed or seriously wounded in this giant of a vehicle, despite some having been on the receiving end of truly massive IEDs. But even it has problems, particularly with the rear axles. The suspension cannot support the enormous weight of extra armour and protection devices added on since its introduction. At one stage the situation with axles was so bad that almost 80 per cent of the Mastiff fleet was out of action because of it. This problem has now largely been rectified with the introduction of a more heavy duty type of axle and better suspension better suited to demanding off road operations.

Force Protection vehicles such as the Mastiff are not expected or designed to be able to cross all of the types of terrain that Afghanistan has, and in many cases the rural roads simply will not support the weight of heavily armoured vehicles. Hence the reason why so many different types of vehicles are deployed on patrols and convoy duty. There have been a number of incidents where heavily armoured vehicles have driven down unsuitable roads, which have quite literally disintegrated under their weight causing the vehicles to overturn. They have even toppled into adjacent canals where the crew have had great difficulty escaping due to the heavy body armour that they are required to wear. It's a trade off. Do you go in heavy, and risk not being able to manoeuvre, which makes you a sitting target or do you go in light and increase your vulnerability to IEDs and RPGs?

Either way, driving around in an armoured vehicle in Afghanistan makes you a bullet magnet for the Taliban. There is no question that since the introduction of Force Protection or MRAP (Mine-Resistant Ambush-Protected) vehicles, as the Americans call them, casualties from roadside IEDs targeted against mounted troops have dropped dramatically. At one time every IED or EFP (Explosively Formed Penetrator) detonated against NATO mounted forces would result in a casualty being sustained, now the Taliban need to carry out eight such attacks to inflict any sort of injury. They are of course masters of tactical innovation, and no doubt will continue to refine and develop their approach to try to gain the upper hand again.

Above: Canadian Coyote on patrol, a vehicle that the Taliban hate as it packs a heavy punch.

Left: Australian convoy on the move.

Above left: 82nd Airborne soldiers dismount from a vehicle in an attempt to engage in conversation with local Afghans – a gesture often appreciated as soldiers riding around in armoured vehicles tend to alienate themselves from what is going on outside.

It is important to stress however that bigger is not always better, as small, lightly armoured vehicles travel too fast for RPGs to engage them effectively. Basically, once a vehicle is travelling at more that 30mph it is very difficult to hit, so therefore the slower, more cumbersome vehicles become the targets instead. Bar or slat armour is often installed on Force protection vehicles – the idea being that the RPG warhead gets trapped between the slats and therefore has no solid surface for it to detonate against. Simple but highly effective.

The idea for these slats is of course not new, as American river monitors and patrol boats operating in the Mekon Delta during the Vietnam War often had them fitted as a low-cost, lightweight means of protecting their crews from RPG attack. Soldiers often wonder why after the Vietnam War this idea did not take off straight away for other uses – such as vehicle protection – as it would seem logical. The answer is that its value was not fully appreciated at the time on account of sailors stating that RPGs were hitting the slats and despite them they were still going off. They however neglected to tell researchers that they had been stuffing the gaps between the slats with sand bags – thereby creating a surface for the RPGs to detonate against, negating the whole concept. Even during the recent Gulf War in Iraq, soldiers were still filling gaps between slats with either extra kit or sand bags – a lesson obviously still not learned in some quarters.

In Afghanistan there is currently a huge drive underway by all NATO members to equip themselves with the latest MRAP vehicles. This is obviously a praiseworthy aim, but what about the psychological implications for the Afghan people? If they see soldiers that are there supposedly to protect them from the Taliban riding around in aggressive looking vehicles bristling with firepower – how can they possibly feel relaxed and reassured that they are safe, when they have nothing? And how also can they build up a rapport with their protectors when they cannot get near to them to communicate? Referring to this problem, one USMC officer said 'What you don't want to do is just stay in your MRAP the entire time. We're trying to separate the insurgency from the population, not ourselves from the population, so it's a bit of a fine line sometimes.' It is analogous to what took place in the UK some years ago with the police, when they decided to ride around in patrol cars instead of walking the beat. The net result was a drop in public confidence, and therefore a major loss of local knowledge and valuable intelligence.

Things of course have now changed, and since introducing the safer neighbourhoods policy, which openly encourages a closer relationship between the public and its protectors the trust is back and therefore the locals work more closely with the police. What's all of this got to do with Afghanistan? A lot I would say, as our soldiers, the ANA and ANP have to start working along similar lines – albeit adjusted and tailored for the Afghan environment. I am not for one second advocating giving back our big force protection vehicles as

Clockwise from top left:
British soldiers from a BRF pose next to their damaged Mastiff, following an IED incident.

A damaged Viking being recovered in the field.

An impressive Oshkosh armoured fuel tanker – however I would not like to be the one driving it around in the Devil's playground.

PWRR Warrior on the move.

A Royal Welsh Warrior complete with bar armour and ECM (electronic counter measures).

Canadian armour preparing to move out.
At the end of 2009, the Canadians were
holding firm. Minister of Foreign Affairs
Laurence Cannon welcomed Obama's
promise of more troops. 'The excellent
co-operation that our military and
civilians enjoy with the US in Kandahar
will certainly be strengthened.'

they are most definitely still needed. It's a question of balance. The goal should be to get to the point where our force protection should be the locals and not armour, as they clearly know who the bad guys are – and where they plant their IEDs and EFPs. They also have a vested interest in helping us, as their families, relatives and friends are just as likely to become victims of these devices as are our own forces. To illustrate this point, during one counter-IED road clearing operation carried out by US combat engineers, the locals saw what they were doing to help them go about their everyday life – and were so impressed that they pointed out where the Taliban usually hid their stash of ready made bombs. This is of course an isolated example, but it should become the norm.

As for the soldiers who drive around in the mighty MRAP vehicles, courses are frequently run in and around their bases to make them aware of exactly where a vehicle can go, and more importantly where it can't. These courses are absolutely vital as between November 2007 and June 2008 there were 66 accidents involving US MRAPs – 40 of which involved rollovers caused by either poor quality roads or weak bridges. They are also taught to read the road they are about to patrol in advance, so that they are well aware of the terrain and likely choke points where vehicle operation is likely to be either restricted or not possible; and more importantly, where IED attack is most likely.

The drivers need to be aware of the height of the vehicles, as they can often snag in overhead wires. Occupants risk the possibility of electrocution – particularly if a communication antenna hits a cable. MRAP vehicles by virtue of their design tend to be unstable on account of their high centre of gravity, which is caused by their blast deflecting V-shaped hulls. Their centre of gravity can also change quickly when they traverse their mounted weapon turrets – particularly on slopes or heavily canted roads – so a lot of thought has to go into the positioning of the vehicle for the safety of the crew.

MRAP represent a logistical challenge. For example, because of their size only a handful of transport aircraft types such as the Boeing C-17 can carry them. Weight is a major problem when planning deployment routes – 70 per cent of the world's bridges cannot support MRAP type vehicles.

A Swedish CV 90 leaves its base on a long range patrol. Hopefully in 2010 the British Army will also have it in service as a replacement for the old and tired Scimitar.

Another problem is transportation costs. To transport an MRAP vehicle by sea from the United States to the Middle-East costs about $13,000 and by air it is a staggering $750,000. That's $250,000 more than it costs to buy one.

Nevertheless, for protection they are vital. Prior to their introduction in Iraq, 63 per cent of all US military losses were IED related. In 2004 the US Marines announced that in over 300 IED attacks on their Cougar MRAPs not one single soldier lost their life. A report in *USA Today* stated that road attacks and troop fatalities in both Iraq and Afghanistan were down by an amazing 99 per cent – with only eight soldiers lost in 2008 in these vehicles. Their introduction has caused the Taliban problems, as to engage these 30 tonne plus monsters they have to build bigger IEDS, which are much more difficult to transport and conceal. Bigger IEDs take longer to set-up, making the setters far more likely to be spotted.

Clockwise from left:

Viking being recovered following an incident; this of course is not always possible in Afghanistan's wilderness.

British Vector, knocked out by IED. Thankfully on this occasion all the occupants survived.

British Vikings on Op Aabi Toorah. This particular vehicle is now being withdrawn from service in Afghanistan, as its protection levels are not up to the threat now being faced by British troops every day.

An American Cougar MRAP (mine resistant ambush protected) undergoing proving trials in the USA. This particular vehicle does exactly what it says on the tin.

MRAP EOD vehicle near Kandahar.

VI

THE REAPERS

In addition to the MRAPs there is another piece of equipment the Taliban detest – the UAV (Unmanned Air Vehicle). Often operating high above the battlefields of Afghanistan and Waziristan, silently and covertly, these unmanned aircraft have the ability to detect and destroy the Taliban and their commanders undetected. Indeed the first tangible proof the world got that the United States had responded to the events of 9/11 came when a CIA-operated Gnat spy UAV was shot down in Afghanistan by the Taliban. This was of course just the beginning.

The UAVs now operating over the crowded airspace of Afghanistan are far more sophisticated and capable than those first seen in 2001. One of their greatest advocates was US Defense Secretary Donald Rumsfeld, who was so impressed with their ability to relay live combat feed from over the battlefield to military commanders within the Pentagon that he insisted upon having it piped into his office. His craze for this Nintendo type of warfare soon became known as 'Rummy TV' – much to the amusement of the US Military. He was however not just a passive viewer, but a player. He would often call up senior US Commanders to demand action when he saw activity that he felt should be either investigated further or terminated. On one occasion he is known to have thrown a major fit when he discovered that a senior Al-Qaeda terrorist commander had escaped being taken out by a precision air strike because US tactical commanders lost precious time seeking official permission for his termination. He fumed 'This is not like asking your ma for permission to leave the dinner table.'

Today not only do UAVs carry out traditional roles such as intelligence gathering, surveillance and reconnaissance, they also act as 'hunter killers.' The US-built General Atomics MQ-9 Reaper is a particularly lethal UAV. This amazing aircraft is capable of either loitering over an area of interest for 14 hours fully laden with stores, or if flying with a smaller weapon load of 1000lbs and carrying 2 1000lb external fuel tanks it can remain airborne for a staggering

42 hours. But that isn't even the most amazing part. It can when operating in the surveillance role read a vehicle number plate from as far away as two miles by means of its thermal camera or if required it can single out an individual's footprint from amongst thousands by means of highly sophisticated sensors. Other capabilities are classified.

At the time of writing the UK operates 2 MQ-9 Reaper UAVs over Afghanistan, both flown by 39 Squadron, RAF, from thousands of miles away in Creech AFB Nevada, near Las Vegas. The men who actually fly them are fully qualified pilots and not arcade gamers. Every time they make a flight decision, 1.2 seconds later, by means of a satellite link, that input is actioned. Why they use qualified pilots is the fact that while operating over Afghanistan they face a multitude of demanding flight challenges – such as icing, shears, and severe turbulence. Only if you are a pilot can you fully understand how demanding such an environment is, and why a high level of skill is required – especially so if a flight system goes unserviceable. The exact rules of combat engagement they have are classified, and where and when they can release ordnance is not a subject that is discussed openly. What we do know however is the type of weaponry available for missions.

Ordnance available includes GBU-12 Paveway 11 Laser Guided Bombs, AGM-114 Hellfire 11 air-to-ground missiles, Aim 9 Sidewinder self-defence air-to-air missiles and in late 2009 they were cleared to drop the GBU-JDAM munition. These UAVs are obviously of immense value, and on the rare occasions that they go rogue or unserviceable, if not recoverable they are destroyed as part of standard denial SOPs. One British MQ-9 Reaper was forced to crash land after a fault developed. Once it was accepted that the aircraft could not be recovered, a special forces team was sent in to destroy it, denying the Taliban any sort of propaganda or material gain. UAVs are politically less controversial than boots on the ground. During the 2009 Pakistani military offensive in the Swat valley, US UAVs operating above the area of operations were able to send back both intelligence and targeting data to the Pakistani forces on the ground – making their lives a lot easier, not to mention safer. Although some elements of Pakistan's government complained about this US involvement over their border, their complaints were nothing compared to what could have happened had US military personnel entered the country. There is also deniability. Nobody except those operating a UAV over a foreign airspace actually know what the full spectrum of their mission is – as opposed to what their government has actually declared. Covert operations can be flown out of Afghanistan over neighbouring countries. It was recently reported that an unknown type of UAV bearing a resemblance to a flying wing was spotted on a NATO airbase in Afghanistan, and then subsequently seen flying over Kandahar.

Although it is public knowledge that such craft known as UCAVs (Unmanned Combat Air Vehicles) are under development in both the US and UK , this

A Canadian mini UAV takes flight – mission unknown.

is the first time that one has been seen flying around over a conflict zone. The type is reported to resemble the Lockheed Pole Cat, but it is of course quite possible that another aircraft manufacturer such as Northrop could be behind it, as they have a tremendous amount of knowledge and experience designing and building flying wings. What mission this particular UAV was flying, is of course another story, but I would lay a bet that US commanders were watching the Taliban's advance towards Pakistan's nuclear facilities and missile storage sites around the clock, prior to them being turned back by the Pakistani Army. At that particular time the United States was providing a great deal of intelligence (and direction) to the Pakistani Government and their military – especially concerning the identification and whereabouts of the Taliban's leadership. A considerable number of Taliban Tier 1 commanders and their lieutenants have been taken out by long endurance armed UAVs loitering around known areas of Taliban activity. These decapitation missions serve to disrupt Taliban command and control and result in major disruptions to their plots and guerrilla war strategy.

These attacks are not just guesswork, but the painstaking result of many weeks of surveillance, often carried out by either special forces or spies within the Taliban itself. Accuracy of weapons selected for such missions is key critical, so precision guided munitions carried on UAVs such as the Reaper need to be literally pinpoint – as collateral damage to innocent civilians has to be avoided at all costs. Indeed, there have been many cases where during the last seconds of an attack, non combatants have inadvertently appeared near a target's location, bringing them within the munitions kill zone. In such circumstances, the mission is terminated and the bomb slewed off target to land in open country. The whole process has to start all over again.

As frustrating as all this is to the UAV pilot concerned, killing civilians has to be avoided at all costs if the hearts and minds of the Afghan people are to be won. When the targets sets are designated to the Reaper operators, a lot of thought has already gone into risk assessing them in advance so that mission scrubs can be avoided. What is particularly amazing about UAV operations over both Afghanistan and Iraq is the sheer number of individual platforms deployed – some 5,500 plus at the last count. Craft employed range in size from the large Reapers which are the hunter killers, down to small, hand-held systems which pack little more than a micro camera. These are normally used by infantry or vehicle patrols as a means of spotting IEDs or possible ambush sites. Under normal circumstances no sane patrol commander would think of deploying from his FOB without some form of UAV coverage; these are life savers.

Unlike the large UAVs, which require a qualified pilot to fly them, the smaller ones need little more than an operator who has good coordination and situational awareness. Particularly intriguing is the command and control element of UAV operations when deployed in the vicinity of other tactical assets such as aircraft and helicopters and the deconfliction issues that must arise with so many platforms flying through what can be a relatively small airspace. Not all of Afghanistan's airspace has radar coverage – especially around the mountain regions. This means that operators have to put a lot of thought into planning their routes, as aside from other airspace users they also have to factor in the dodging of artillery barrages and air strikes called in by troops following a contact.

As effective as the current generation of UAVs are in Afghanistan, even more are planned to enter service in the next few years. These will range from micro spy craft designed to fly into compounds covertly to locate booby traps and enemy positions in advance of an assault, to aircraft-size UCAVs, which will have full autonomy to release ordnance on Taliban targets already desig-nated in advance by surveillance UAVs.

The UK has changed its attitude towards UAVs. Back in the 1990s the UK's interest and experience in this area was limited to say the least, with our only fielded surveillance platform being the Phoenix – the subject of great ridicule for both our armed forces and those of our allies. They simply could not believe that a platform that cost so much money to develop could perform so badly.

Our US friends were also slightly confused as to why we had embarked down this sorry road, when they had offered us their highly effective Predator, which was at the time state-of-the-art and far more affordable. Now, the UK is a major player in the UAV world, both in terms of experience and platforms operated. Indeed at the time of writing, BAE are about to start flight testing their new Mantis UAV, which is in terms of weapons and sensors carriage a UK equivalent to the MQ-9 Reaper. Mantis is being pursued as a means of deliv-ering a UK sovereign capability, as we are at this present time currently too dependent on overseas manufacturers for our present operational platforms. It promises the ability to operate at up to 55,000ft – for intelligence gathering, surveillance, reconnaissance, target acquisition and close air support. Mantis is also being designed to carry the L-3 Wescam MX-20 HD electro-optical/infrared sensor and the Selex Galileo synthetic aperture radar.

Some of the sensors currently being developed for use in Afghanistan are mightily impressive. I was shown an aerial photo of members of the public walking in front of the Houses of Parliament in London, which showed their faces and even what newspapers they were carrying. When asked how far away it was taken to give such clarity, I guessed around 500 feet. I was slightly out, as the platform that took the photograph was flying off the UK coastline – 80 miles away. They then told me that this was relatively old technology and that they had cameras under development that featured over 100 mil-lion pixels. As impressive as Mantis is, an even more sophisticated platform

Left: The face of the future. A manned USMC Harrier with an unmanned USAF UAV.

Above left: MQ-9 Reaper.

Above: MQ1 Predator with Hellfires.

is under development, known as the Taranis. Although a UCAV rather than a UAV, this system will offer a quantum leap in capability. Its payload, speed and manoeuvrability are more that of a conventional fighter/bomber than that of a simple, slow moving unmanned aircraft. Although both of these platforms are still some way off from entering service with the RAF, they're in the post.

Until their arrival, the RAF has expressed a desire to field as many as 13 Reapers, but with the current defence budget pressures in the UK, this seems unlikely to happen. One thing is for sure though, the Reapers that the RAF do have are doing a great job, and because of this and the work of the other UAVs that are in operation over Afghanistan, British soldiers and their allies are a lot safer.

VII

THE GOLDEN HOUR

It is often said that the first hour following a major trauma is the most important, if the casualty is to survive. And nowhere is this more evident than on the battlefields of Afghanistan, where the survival clock is always ticking down. That said, a recent surgeon operating out of the excellent medical facilities in Camp Bastion, Helmand, stated in a recent interview 'If you're going to get seriously injured anywhere in the world today, you could not pick a better place to improve your chances of survival than Afghanistan today. Where else could you have as many as four top surgeons operating on you at the same time? Answer, nowhere.' He was referring to one of the few positive aspects of this war – the modern miracle of combat medicine.

This war has seen some of the greatest ground-breaking medical advances in recent years, with more being developed on the battlefield itself. New treatments are being born out of combat experiences as they take place, with new procedures quickly following. Some aspects of treatment and care will no doubt find a place outside the military world.

In the early days of UK involvement in the Afghan conflict post 9/11 the standard practice following the report of casualties was to send a helicopter out to wherever the incident was and then to recover them back to a medical facility. Today however, assuming that the landing zone nearest to where the casualty lies is cleared – 'not hot' – then the operating theatre will be coming to them, usually in the back of a Chinook. As you can imagine, sending a Chinook out with four crew – plus a highly skilled medical team and their escorts, usually around 12 personnel – is in itself a significant risk.

That said, if such a mission can be flown, the chances of the injured victim surviving are significantly higher. There have been a number of occasions where soldiers have incurred horrific injuries that only a few years ago would not have been survivable but today they can if given the full trauma suite treatment in time. What most people forget when they read of casualties being sustained in Afghanistan is that for every soldier killed, there are five

Clockwise from left:

ISAF and Afghan forces practise helicopter medical evacuation procedures, a skill that they are almost certainly going to have to use for real at some point or other during their respective tours of duty.

British soldiers load one of their wounded colleagues on to a US Black Hawk helicopter for treatment at Camp Bastion.

British medics practise their art in advance of their deployment to Afghanistan, courtesy of the Afghan training village in Norfolk.

Troops board a Hercules at Camp Bastion.

Med Tech L/Cpl Michael Birkett (RAMC) takes a well-deserved break after a long patrol in Lashkar Gah.

seriously injured. Hence my appeal at the beginning of this book. Why are so many surviving? That's down to three main reasons.

Today soldiers serving in the front line are issued with highly effective body armour that is capable of stopping high-velocity rounds, significantly reducing the risk of chest injuries. Soldiers also wear helmets that greatly reduce the risk of head wounds caused by gunshots and blasts. Also it is increasingly common to see soldiers wearing ballistic eye protection, which aside from providing anti glare can also protect them from flying stones and blast debris.

In addition to their own personal protective kit, soldiers also carry one-handed tourniquets and special bandages impregnated with clotting agents, which greatly help reduce loss of blood following a severe injury. Known as Quikclot, this powdery substance consisting of porous minerals called zeolites is poured directly into a wound to staunch the bleeding.

Another fascinating product is the hemostatic bandage, which contains chitin molecules from shrimp shells that become extremely adhesive when they make contact with blood. These amazing items combined together stop bleeding and seal wounds, thereby buying more time until a Forward Surgical Team intervenes, be it on board a CASEVAC helicopter or at a medical facility at a COB (Contingency Operating Base).

Thirdly, once the Forward Surgical Team has done its job – entailing damage control, surgery and rehabilitation – the casualty is off to the next level of care. This usually involves the casualty being flown by a Critical Care Air Transport Team back to either the UK or Lanstuhl in Germany for more specialised treatment. Treatment is now so advanced and integrated that a specialist surgeon based in Los Angeles for instance can by means of a video link supervise a procedure in Germany or even Afghanistan if required. A detailed trauma register is also maintained so that injuries can be analyzed, thereby helping in the development of better and more effective treatments.

The Future

As impressive as all these treatments are, even more spectacular procedures and practices are under development. For instance, blood loss, normally a major reason for loss of life, may not be such a major problem, as a powdered blood is currently under development for use in Afghanistan. When it enters service, in the not too distant future, all you will have to do is add saline water – and hey presto, instant blood.

Another piece of kit currently being developed for use in Afghanistan is the focused ultrasound, a device that will heat and coagulate blood in an internal wound. This particular device will be invaluable to Army medics and surgeons as internal injuries are often very difficult to both detect and treat. One can only marvel at some of these future developments, as fatalities are already plummeting in comparison to previous wars, despite the lethality of modern weaponry. The survival rate for a soldier injured in Afghanistan is currently 90 per cent or higher, a significant improvement over the 1991 Gulf War.

Another interesting statistic relates to our combat losses. We now lose far fewer soldiers in combat then we would if they were back in their barracks or on leave. In the UK alone we have lost 1,748 service personnel since 1990 in non-combat related accidents and incidents, whereas our combat casualties in both Iraq and Afghanistan are only a fraction of this. Statistically speaking, and thanks to modern combat medicine, you are far safer in a conflict zone than you would be if you were garrisoned back in the UK. Bizarre but true.

Rehabilitation

One other area which is truly inspirational concerns those that have been seriously injured in Afghanistan and their determination to get back to normal life. For them rehabilitation starts almost as soon as they enter the recovery phase of their treatment. Injuries treated by physiotherapy include multiple fractures, amputation, loss of sight or hearing, brain injury and often, sadly, a combination of them. In the UK, Selly Oak is the main rehabilitation centre, with a worldwide reputation for excellence. Here they often pioneer new treatments, one of which is mirror therapy – used to treat amputees with phantom limb pain (PLP). PLP occurs when the nerve endings at the base of the amputation deceive the brain into believing that the amputated limb is still there.

With mirror therapy, an amputee using a mirror box can mirror the missing limb – thereby tricking the brain. This involves exercising the existing limb while watching the movement in the mirror. The reflection seen creates the illusion of two limbs moving together – tricking the brain into believing that there are still two limbs, which has the net effect of overriding any mismatched nerve signals that are being sent. Genius.

New Body Parts

As impressive as our medical advances in Afghanistan are today, there is a treatment currently under development in the United States that if successful, will push medical science beyond recognition – almost into the realms of science fiction: the regrowth of body parts. There is a real possibility of a soldier growing back his lost digits, feet, arms, legs and even ears.

Sounds too good to be true, but if America's military research arm DARPA (Defense Advanced Research Project Agency) is successful in its current human regeneration project then this will be reality in a matter of years. Currently, if a soldier loses a hand or limb, the only treatment on offer is the fitting of a prosthetic one. Yet scientifically, it is possible to regenerate. It has been found that a certain type of salamander has the amazing ability to regenerate its body parts, such as legs, in a matter of days.

Certain parts taken from a pig and impregnated into a human body in dust form causes it to be populated by stem cells resulting in regeneration. We humans do have an embryonic ability to regenerate during the early stages of our development, but for some reason it stops after a certain period. The trick is now to find a way of getting the body to regenerate again on a larger scale. The powder is currently known as Pixie Dust – and has just been used for the first time on a human.

The soldier who has agreed to trial this treatment is US Army Sgt Shiloh Harris, who suffered very serious facial injuries and the loss of a number of his fingers. Although still early days, one of his fingers currently being treated has already started to grow back – much to his amazement. While there is still more work to be done of course, the possibility of being able to grow limbs back could be only a decade or so away. This is just one of many treatments that are currently being developed for our wounded soldiers, and no doubt many more will follow as a direct consequence of the Afghan conflict.

An 82nd Airborne soldier scopes out suspicious movement from a ridge above his position.

Left to right:

Soldiers from 1st Battalion Welsh Guards fix bayonets, prior to assaulting a Taliban compound.

A Royal Marine from 42 CDO engages a target with an 84mm LAW.

42 Commando, Royal Marines on patrol in a hot and dusty area of Helmand Province.

Clockwise from top:

US soldiers prepare to storm a house – always highly dangerous work as an IED could await them on the other side of the door.

Gurkha Limbu reacting to an ambush.

Capturing the moment an artillery shell leaves the barrel of a US 155mm gun.

A British soldier shows some captured hash following a raid in a local bazaar.

VIII

THE DEVIL'S PLAYGROUND

In my last book *Battlefield Afghanistan*, I finished with 'As for NATO, they are going to be in Afghanistan for a very long time to come. And assuming all goes well, their role will switch from direct conflict to reconstruction and security, but that's clearly only going to be after some very serious fighting is done. The most troubling thing is that I do not think we have seen the worst of it yet. I do believe that we will prevail in the long run. But it will be, in the words of Wellington, "the most desperate business".' That was written in late 2006, and here we are more than three years later and the tempo of operations and the intensity of combat experienced by our forces is as fierce as ever. There has however been a complete shift in the Taliban's tactics – as today they wage war primarily by means of the IED (Improvised Explosive Device). And they are rather good at it.

The IED Threat

In 2008, there were 3,276 IED attacks – 45 per cent up on the previous year. In the first two months of 2009 alone, 36 coalition soldiers lost their lives to IEDs. However, in July 2009 the Taliban surpassed themselves when they mounted a staggering 828 IED attacks – of which 108 were successful. This resulted in the loss of 49 coalition soldiers. They called it Bloody July.

To try and put these figures into perspective: when British forces first entered Helmand in 2006, our detection rate for IEDs was around 40 per cent, whereas today with better search kit and more specialist personnel deployed it has risen to an impressive 80 per cent. But more needs to be done of course to raise the detection rates even further. To this end NATO must adopt some of the best practices developed in Iraq, such as those of the US Task Force ODIN (Observe, Detect, Identify and Neutralise) programme, which was developed

Two A10s loiter above the killing fields of Afghanistan, in anticipation of a possible mission. The Thunderbolts are often called in to provide a show of force and their arrival alone can be enough to prompt a retreat or a cessation of hostilities on the part of the Taliban.

Afghan Air Corps helicopters on the flight line in Kabul.

to win back the roads from IED placement teams by using a combination of manned and unmanned platforms to perform reconnaissance, surveillance and target acquisition (RSTA) missions over key road systems.

Task Force ODIN is very different in its approach to countering the IED threat than other strategies in that it takes an offensive approach to the problem rather than a defensive one, such as the building of bigger and heavier MRAP type vehicles. It is far better to disrupt the IED networks before they get a chance to target forces than it is to try and deal with devices that have already been planted. NATO are not the only ones developing new tactics all the time; the Taliban are also getting more sophisticated in their methods. For example, nowadays they rarely use explosives in their devices, instead they rely on other materials such as organic peroxide – which is both easily acquired and far more devastating than TNT – as its blast wave has three times the range. Their means of detonation are becoming ever more sophisticated, with a shift towards more remote-based technology such as the use of high-powered cordless phones, the base stations of which can be positioned some 50km away from the handset. Active and passive infrared (IR) devices are also becoming popular, but they have their limitations.

What is not often appreciated is just how efficient and clever the Taliban bombers are. For instance, as soon as our soldiers leave their FOBs to go out on patrol they screen their route in advance for IEDs which is a required SOP. But barely have they completed this task, and you guessed it, the Taliban have planted IEDs on the very route they have just cleared. Their methods are not always obvious. They will send a lone, unarmed operator along a path with a wheelbarrow containing wood or materials that at first glance would give a soldier searching them little cause for concern. This will then be followed up by others taking the same route, who again individually have nothing on them that would cause alarm. It is only when they put their individual items together that you get any idea what they are up to – and by then it is often too late.

They often deliberately leave suspicious items near paths used by our soldiers so as to cause them delay. Meanwhile, as the counter IED teams are going about their dangerous business, the Taliban are busy nearby planting a real IED near to a place already cleared earlier in the day. This ploy is particularly effective, because even if an alert soldier spots it and calls it in, there is always a danger that someone may think it has already been cleared safe, as they have seen search teams in the same location earlier on.

Other ploys are used against coalition vehicle patrols operating off-road. What will often happen is again simple but effective. Typically a patrol will be shadowed by an unarmed Taliban fighter on a motorbike, whose job is to follow them and try and anticipate where they are going. Once he has a rough idea of their likely intended route, he contacts his colleagues who will try and either block their route or force them to alter it. This can be done in a subtle way such as by blocking the route with lots of animals or more overtly by leaving a vehicle that looks extremely suspect. Either way, most patrols will try and avoid such situations as they fear that they are being set up for an ambush – which will usually mean they will change their route; which is exactly what the Taliban want. At this particular point they will have laid IEDs along all other possible routes of advance, creating a perfect ambush opportunity. The Taliban are aware of the fact that British soldiers are particularly vulnerable to IED attack as they do not have enough helicopters in theatre to transport them. The only way for them to get about is either on foot or by vehicle.

The following statement was made by Lt Col Rupert Thorneloe during a confidential commanders' briefing given on June 5 2009. His thoughts are particularly poignant – as he was killed barely a month later, on July 1, by a roadside IED while travelling in a convoy in Helmand.

> I have tried to avoid griping about helicopters – we all know we don't have enough. We cannot not move people, so this month we have conducted a great deal of administrative movement by road, this increases the IED threat and our exposure to it.

Lt Col Rupert Thorneloe was the most senior British soldier to have lost his life in Afghanistan. By all accounts he was a very brave and courageous man who always led his soldiers from the front. Sadly, we are losing far too many like him.

The Battle For The Blades

Picking up on Lt Col Thorneloe's comments relating to the lack of helicopter support in Afghanistan, he is of course not the only senior officer to have expressed such a point of view. The number of people with the same thoughts is growing all the time. There is a problem: the British government just do not accept the fact that their forces in the region are under-resourced in helicopters, pointing to the fact that the fleet has almost tripled since they first deployed to Helmand Province. This is true, but what they neglect to mention is the fact that our troop numbers in Afghanistan have significantly increased also – meaning that in real terms our soldiers are now actually worse off than they were before. The opinions of senior military commanders and the politicians could not be more polarised.

Military, June 5 – 'We all know we haven't enough helicopters.' PM Gordon Brown, July 22 – 'It's completely wrong to say that the loss of lives has been

Clockwise from right:

Bravo Company Black Watch on patrol in Helmand.

ANA gunners carry out their first live fire with a heavy gun under the watchful eyes of an Italian mentoring team.

An Afghan pilot proudly poses in front of his aircraft after graduating flight school in Kabul.

RAF Chinook over the Red Desert.

Black Watch meeting Extraction Force One.

caused by the absence of helicopters'. The same month 22 British soldiers were killed in Afghanistan, most killed by IEDs. If we contrast our current helicopter situation in Afghanistan with that of Iraq, I cannot ever recall hearing of any significant problems regarding either their numbers or capabilities.

Compare that to a report regarding UK helicopter support, marked classified 'NATO Secret' in which it was stated that UK helicopter operations in Afghanistan were 'not fit for purpose'. This particular document was leaked to the British *Daily Mail* newspaper – which for operational security reasons would not reveal any further classified details of problems associated with helicopter support capability, as it could endanger our forces. But elsewhere in the report, which was submitted by Lt Col Thorneloe, he mentions that at times he had virtually no helicopters of the type that would be needed to move his troops by air rather than by road. 'The current level of SH (support helicopters) support is therefore unsustainable.' He concluded by saying that the system used to manage helicopter movements in Afghanistan 'is very clearly not fit for purpose'. Yet in Iraq he observed that they 'were managed in a more flexible, efficient manner.'

In another report submitted in July 2009, a senior officer also observed that operational movements had been hampered by lack of helicopter support. In his case there was only a 50 per cent availability, which again meant more IED exposure for his troops. 'Aviation has been erratic throughout this week. This has forced us to conduct more road moves than I would like. I understand the strains in the fly programme but any improvements would greatly assist.' It was also around this time that just prior to his retirement General Sir Richard Dannatt, while on his final official visit to Afghanistan in July 2009, commented upon the lack of availability of suitable helicopter assets in Afghanistan, which as you can imagine ruffled a few feathers within the Government. At one stage Sir Richard found himself without a ride from the RAF and had to hitch a lift in a US Black Hawk helicopter, thereby proving his point. But that wasn't the worst part of this embarrassing episode. Upon his return to the UK it was revealed that Sikorsky, the manufacturers of the Black Hawk helicopter, had at the same time been involved in an eleventh hour meeting with the MoD to supply the British Forces with this particular model. They rejected it. It was not the first time that Sikorsky had been in talks with the MoD to supply Black Hawks. They have now made three attempts.

The first of these occurred in 2007, when Sikorsky offered the UK 60 Black Hawk UH-60 Model Ls including aircrew training for $480m – which in relative terms and by defence standards was a fantastic deal. It was rejected. This decision surprised everyone, as 30 helicopters would have been supplied off the production line in 2008, which would have solved the problems in an instant. The other 30 were to follow later in the year. As our transport woes continued in Afghanistan, Sikorsky came back with a second offer in 2008.

They offered the UK 12 S 70 Black Hawks – half to be supplied in 2011 with the remainder delivered in 2012; again, rejected.

Then in June 2009, they made yet another offer, this time for 60 Black Hawk M Models – 5 to be delivered in 2010, 13 in 2011 and the rest by staggered delivery with completion aimed at 2013. Again this was rejected, much to the dismay of our armed forces who thought it was a done deal. The Americans were also extremely disappointed as they felt that their offer was very good, and made more sense as it meant that both the UK and the US forces in Afghanistan would be operating the same platforms, thus saving money in operational costs. So what great deal did the UK opt for instead? As amazing as it sounds a decision was taken to patch up and refurbish 28 forty-year-old RAF Puma helicopters – which were due to be scrapped in 2011. The cost of this option was a staggering $300m. To be fair, I should point out that the helicopters will get new engines and flight instrumentation – plus a lick of paint. But does it represent good value? An emphatic no, as each of the 28 Pumas – nicknamed the Albatross by the RAF – will cost $10.7m each to refurbish, and will have a service life of some ten years. Earliest delivery estimate for the Puma is 2011. Had we taken advantage of the Black Hawk deal offered in 2007, our armed forces would now have 60 of them in service – at a cost of $7.5m each. And they would have a service life of some 40 years.

There is also the question of survivability. The Black Hawk has been built from the outset to absorb punishment and is the ultimate battlefield survivor. The chairman of the House of Commons Select Defence Committee, James Arbuthnot, speaking in a recent interview given after condemning the Puma decision, stated that it had 'poor survivability in combat'. This old museum piece is going to be flying British soldiers over one of the most hostile environments in the world. When the Puma first entered service in 1971, it was for its time a good helicopter, and still acquits itself well in the civilian world, especially as an oil rig support platform. But for Afghanistan, it's just not the right tool for the job So just who is to blame for this helicopter fiasco?

My personal view is Number 10, and indirectly Britain's closest allies, the United States. Why? Because they constantly keep bailing out the Brits by lending them their own helicopters. It means the Government can avoid any expenditure for a little while longer. At the end of 2009 in Afghanistan, a British officer was assigned as an air operations controller to a US unit about to commence a major operation. When he arrived the CO of the American unit asked him how many British helicopters he had brought with him. The reply was 'None, we plan to use yours.' And they did.

In the not too distant future, there will be a slight improvement in British SH assets in Afghanistan with the arrival of six RAF Merlins – that are currently on work-up training. It has to be said that the Merlin is eagerly awaited by British troops, as its performance in Iraq was deemed excellent. Also a

An Australian soldier out on patrol across Afghanistan's hot and dusty plains.

number of extra Chinooks will be deployed to bolster the current ones that are providing sterling service in Helmand. There are of course a small number of Lynx utility helicopters in country also, but they can only operate effectively during the winter months, as their engines struggle to deal with the hot and high conditions of Afghanistan during the summer months. In addition to these platforms, there are also a small number of Sea Kings in theatre, which, although not spectacular in performance, do provide some stop-gap capability until the arrival of more suitable assets.

Hopefully, three years hence, the bad memory of lack of support helicopters will have faded.

The Unbroken Square

Even in the darkest days of this conflict – and there have been plenty of them – the troops have never wavered. I compare their attitude to that shown by Wellington's soldiers at the Battle of Waterloo – where all believed that at some point their fellows in some other regiment may well fail to perform as well as they should – but it would certainly never be them that let the side down. I think that is the strength of the British Army. Every regiment and corps believes that it is the best, and their colleagues a close second. Every soldier believes that he or she is the consummate professional and that it will be someone somewhere else who will let the side down – but not them.

It almost harks back to the old days when soldiers formed squares to resist cavalry attacks – knowing full well that if one person broke, then somebody else would follow, until eventually the square broke. And although tactics, uniform and equipment may have changed, the British soldier of today is still the same as ever. The finest bar none.

Creeping Doubts

I mention these qualities, because to be frank there are other members of NATO who, if faced with the same magnitude of combat that the British forces have had to endure, would have either buckled or their politicians withdrawn them. The three NATO members who are enduring the lion's share of this conflict are the United States, the UK and Canada – who will leave in 2010 if some Canadian politicians get their way. Obviously, behind the scenes both the US and UK governments are trying to persuade them to stay onside, as they are an extremely valuable ally both militarily and politically. In sheer numbers, the US could of course replace their force in a moment. But there might be a domino effect. If Canada wavers, then who will be next? There are a small number of other NATO members who are also beginning to waver. Part of this doubt stems from the fact that there does not appear to be a consistent workable strategy for Afghanistan, and the arrival of a new ISAF commander spells change yet again.

For many it is dawning upon them that although their soldiers face a constant threat from the Taliban in Afghanistan, their homelands face no such threat from them directly, as the Taliban are only active in Afghanistan and Pakistan and have no apparent international desires. At times, there seems to be great confusion as to what we are actually fighting for. If we turn back to the dark days after 9/11, the West went to Afghanistan to engage those disciples of terror who were busy within the training camps of Al-Qaeda planning and working up in preparation for their next terrorist outrage. It just so happened that the Taliban decided to protect them, as they deemed us enemies (and infidels) because we had invaded Afghanistan.

Does that mean that the West may have got the strategy wrong? Could they have actually negotiated with the Taliban for the expulsion of Al-Qaeda without having to fight them? It does present mind boggling possibilities and questions. If we are really honest and look back on Afghanistan's history, the West showed little or no interest in Afghanistan from the time the Soviets were evicted in 1989 right up until September 11 2001. The West didn't really give a damn about what was going in Afghanistan during that period. But it sure started caring when Al-Qaeda started to attack from there.

Maybe after the events of 9/11 the war should have been fought by means of special forces operating through a surrogate force who had a vested interest in fighting. After all, that is what happened in 2001/2002 when the West initially fought the Taliban through the efforts of the Northern Alliance – a proxy force. And by any benchmark this working relationship was extremely successful, as it caused little resentment amongst the Afghan people or indeed at home – as precious few at the time even knew of our involvement in this war. That is the key advantage of special forces-type operations – their deniability. As to casualties, by definition you cannot possibly sustain many, as you do not have that many soldiers on the ground to become them. So many US Senators are now advocating their use in place of conventional forces.

They are however a tad late, as the West has already committed itself to the protection of the Afghan people and it cannot and must not let them down. So where do we go from here with the Taliban? We are now approaching something of a political crossroads in Afghanistan. So whisper it – the West needs to need to make efforts to engage with the more moderate elements amongst them – who are also looking for a way out of this mess. It should be remembered that the Pakistanis have on a number of occasions arranged successful

B1 taking on extra fuel after a long range patrol. These aircraft can cover enormous distances very quickly and have the ability to delivery lethal ordnance with pinpoint accuracy.

British troops exiting a hot Chinook.

ceasefires with the Taliban. Life is certainly not easy for them, as they have lost an estimated third of their operational fighting strength during 2009. For every soldier NATO loses in Afghanistan, they lose 20. In July that year, they lost well over 200 of their number while engaging British forces in Helmand alone. But these numbers pale in comparison with the casualties they took while fighting the Pakistani Army in the Swat valley.

Reliable Taliban casualty figures are of course hard to come by outside of reports by ISAF forces, but we can be sure of one thing. They are coming off worst almost every time. The Taliban is not a nihilist group hell-bent on global jihad – like their Al-Qaeda friends – they are essentially a national movement composed of disparate tribal leaders and local followers who are united in their hatred of the foreign invaders. They are also not stupid. If some form of workable political roadmap could be put in front of them, that gave them a way out without losing face, many of them would take it. Indeed, there are many who have already switched sides, mostly as a result of financial inducements it has to be said. But it's a start.

A deal was made with the insurgents in Basra, Iraq, that for the most part held. The Taliban leader Mullah Omar once gave serious consideration to handing over Osama bin Laden to the Saudi security forces as a means of winning political favour but his colleagues talked him out of it. It does show that they can be brought around. Perhaps in the near future another opportunity will arise to strike a deal, following the major Pakistani military offensive launched against the Taliban in Waziristan in October 2009.

This offensive was the biggest of its kind yet, and involved some 30,000 troops, supported by air assets – both Pakistani and American – assaulting Waziristan. In addition to the Pakistani offensive, US special forces and local converted Waziris are also engaging the Taliban from inside Waziristan, which means the Taliban are fighting a war on two fronts, both in Afghanistan and Pakistan. And anyone who knows anything about warfare will tell you that if you try and fight a war on two fronts you need two things – piles of ammunition and piles of body bags.

The fact that some of the Waziri tribes along with others elsewhere have now turned against them – with a little help of course from the CIA and US special forces – is a very significant development. The apparent simplicity of this strategy is misleading. The idea of turning tribes is of course nothing new, as it was done in Iraq as a matter of routine, and with great success. In fact it had more effect on calming the Iraqi situation than any surge of troops ever achieved. In its most simple form, to bring about change in tribal attitude all you need to do is offer them money according to the level of security in their tribal region. The more peaceful the region, the more money and assistance the area gets. This of course means that in order to get the aid, they need to get rid of unwanted guests – the Taliban. Most of the time they go quietly, hoping that they can return another time, but there have been occasions when they have fought their former hosts. On October 10 2008 for example, the Taliban beheaded four tribal leaders because they were pro-government. But that wasn't their worst outrage. On October 11 2008, a suicide bomber was sent in to attack an anti-Taliban gathering that involved tribal elders planning an attack against a local militant base. The result of this lethal car bomb attack was 110 dead and 125 wounded.

To understand why the Taliban were now taking such a hard line you would have to go back to the previous month, in which some 30,000 tribesmen had pledged to fight the Taliban following the displacement of around 300,000 people as a result of the clashes between the Taliban and the Pakistani military. Indeed, so committed were the tribal elders to driving the Taliban out they threatened that anyone who gave the Taliban sanctuary would be fined one million rupees and have their house torched. As encouraging as these stories are, there is still an awful long way to go before all the tribal leaders are on side. If the Taliban need any more signs that change is in the air, here's one more. Opium poppy growth is now dramatically down compared to previous bumper years. There are two main reasons. The opium market is now saturated, so prices have crashed. And the alternative crops such as wheat now have more value, so poppy farmers are switching. Most of the Taliban's income is derived from the proceeds of opium poppy growth. No money means no ability to fight.

Afghan Security Forces

Who is going to provide security for the people of Afghanistan once NATO eventually withdraws after the pacification of the Taliban? Currently the plan is that both the Afghan National Army and the Afghan Police will be the providers of security, but both still have some way to go before they are proficient enough to undertake this role.

Afghan National Army

As of December 2008 its strength was 79,000, of which some 52,000 were actually engaged in combat operations. Its current ORBAT is 5 Corps HQs, one mechanized brigade HQ, 13 light brigade HQs with 72 combat, combat support, service support and commando battalions. To give some idea of its effectiveness, in 2007 the ANA led some 45 per cent of military operations in Afghanistan, but by spring 2008 this figure had risen to an impressive 62 per cent. As of November 2008 its fighting capability was assessed as follows:

Above: Dutch troops bedding down for the night.

Above right: CH46E Sea Knight prior to its operational retirement from Afghanistan.

Right: F15E fast mover taking on fuel. During a war in which NATO/ISAF have expressly stated that the winning of the support of the Afghan people is paramount, is the use of such lethal stand-off hardware actually counterproductive? Is it, quite literally, overkill, as some have argued? ISAF ground forces would not agree.

CM1 (capable of operational independence) – seven battalions, one brigade and one corps HQ.

CM2 (capable of planning, executing, and sustaining counter insurgency operations at battalion level with ISAF support) – 29 battalions/squadrons, six brigade HQs and three corps HQs.

CM3 (partially capable of conducting counter insurgency operations at the company level with support from ISAF) – 25 battalions/squadrons, four brigade HQs, one corps HQ and the ANA Air Corps HQ.

CM4 (formed but not yet capable of conducting primary operational missions) – six battalions/squadrons and one brigade HQ.

CM5 (planned but still not formed or reporting) – 18 battalions/squadrons and two brigade HQs.

The two units that are capable of independent operations at company level are the 201st and 203rd Corps. The ANA is also currently building up its own support assets, and at the time of writing has a number of artillery, mortar, recce, engineer and logistics units that are operationally deployable.

One of the key aspects of NATO's strategy for Afghanistan is that the ANA should grow in number and capability in order to relieve its forces on the ground that are engaged in direct combat operations. To that end the plan is to increase the ANA to a strength of 134,000 by 2011 – perhaps 175,000 if more money and support can be provided. This will of course involve restructuring the ANA to a new ORBAT as follows:

Five Corps HQs with commando units
One Capital divisional HQ
18 Light brigade HQs
One Mechanized brigade HQ
One Commando brigade HQ
One Service and security support brigade HQ
114 Combat, combat support, combat service support and commando battalions.
19 Garrison support battalions.

Of particular interest is the commando battalions, formed to enhance the ANA's strike capability. Eventually these units will of course produce some form of special forces capability.

Afghan Army Air Corps

Supporting the Afghan National Army, the Afghan Army Air Corps is growing in capability by the day. At present it has 301 fully trained pilots, who are part of an organisation that aspires to grow to a projected strength of some 7,400 personnel operating a fleet of 126 aircraft. Types currently operated and planned include:

61 Mi-17 transport helicopters
58 Mi-17 troop transport helicopters
Three Mi-17 VIP helicopters
9 Mi-35 attack helicopters
20 C-27 transport aircraft
6 AN 32 aircraft
2 AN-26 aircraft
28 turboprop light strike aircraft

But as good as the ANA and AAAC are, they are not police, nor should they be employed as such. So all aspects of civil policing and law enforcement is going to be down to the Afghan National Police.

Afghan National Police

At this present time they are just not up to the job. ISAF's desired target of 82,000 officers is still some way short as there are only 76,000 potential officers currently registered. So as to have some sort of standard measurement of capability, ISAF has introduced the capability milestone (CM) qualification – with 1 being the best possible standard for a police unit to aspire to. As of November 2008, this was the status of the Afghan National Police.

18 units had achieved CM1
16 units had achieved CM2
22 units had achieved CM3
317 units had achieved CM4

So there was plenty of room for improvement and there still is. Not helping matters is the fact that there is a serious shortage of both US and ISAF qualified police instructors. Currently, the vast majority of international instructors come from the US Marine Corps – some 1,200. But more outside expertise is still needed.

Another major issue concerns anti-corruption policing protocol, which requires officers to be linked up to an internet-based reporting system. This is fine for a western force, but in Afghanistan the vast majority of officers cannot

USAF F15E commencing attack on Taliban.

read or write, so this system is currently unworkable. Also there is fraud at local police stations, where wages are paid out. In a bid to stop this, all officers will be paid from a central location, from which their salaries will be paid directly into their bank accounts as would be the case in the West. Another issue concerns the exploitation of local communities where the officer is known – a common problem in rural areas where everyone knows everyone. To avoid this problem, officers cannot serve in the area where they are from.

One other sensitive issue is female police officers. In male-dominated Afghanistan their introduction into the Afghan National Police has been very controversial. Currently they have one instructor who is from the UK MoD police, and by all accounts she is making good progress with them. At the time of writing, the Afghan National Police is organised within:

365 Districts
46 City Police Precincts
34 Provinces
Six Regions
20 ANCOP Battalions
33 Afghan Border Police Battalions
135 Afghan Border Police Companies.

It is going to be a long time before the Afghan Police Force gets up to western standards – if ever.

As if confidence in the Afghan National Police was not already low enough in ISAF, an incident on November 3 2009 plummeted it even further. The cause of this collapse was the slaughter by an Afghan police officer of five British soldiers who were serving as his mentors at a check point in Helmand province. In addition to the five killed, a further six soldiers were also seriously injured as well as a number of loyal Afghan police officers.

What is truly shocking about this incident is the fact that the individual involved was known to have connections to the Taliban and yet nobody took any action. It is not the first time that an Afghan police officer has killed ISAF soldiers, as two US soldiers were killed by another rogue officer the previous month while out on patrol in Wardak. In fact, there were six incidents in 2009 where NATO forces have come under attack from men wearing Afghan security uniforms, though some of these are now known to have been stolen.

All ISAF mentoring personnel are regularly reminded that there is always a chance that one of their subjects could go rogue – but it is always a terrible thing when someone you thought was trustworthy turns a gun on you. In the words of Dr Andrew Wilder, Research Director at Tufts University, US, additional resources should not be wasted but 'contribute to the development of an Afghan police force that will act as 'cops' rather than 'robbers'.

The Way Forward

Throughout this chapter I have outlined a lot of theoretical what ifs and made some assumptions as to possible ways forward. These are of course only my opinions – but they are based on facts and known givens that if combined together could form the basis of an exit strategy. Many would disagree with me and state that we should just keep on fighting until something gives. But that does not really make any sense. If we look back on the experience of southern Iraq, the military top brass eventually admitted their forces were making the situation worse by just being there. When the British withdrew back to their main base outside Basra the situation calmed almost immediately. There have of course been the odd harassment attacks – but they are a mere fraction of what they used to be. If you ask me if this is now the situation in Afghanistan, I would sadly agree.

From 2001 to 2006 the British lost just five soldiers in Afghanistan, since then, in the last three years losses have increased to 237 as of 7 December 2009. The British are not alone in this, as US and Canadian losses have also increased substantially. This is why President Obama took so long to make the big decision on whether to surge troop numbers in Afghanistan or reduce them. No doubt weighing on his mind was the conclusion of one of his most senior officials – former US Marine Captain Matthew Hoh – who resigned in protest at the way in which the war was being conducted. He believed the NATO presence was actually emboldening the insurgency, as the Pashtun tribes of Afghanistan – who make up most of the Taliban – saw our troops as being part of 'a continued and sustained assault, going back centuries, on Pashtun land, culture, traditions and religion'.

His views are backed up by the results of a late 2009 poll, which found that only 45 per cent of the Afghan population in southern Afghanistan supported the NATO presence, whereas the year before it was 83 per cent. The Afghan elections – riddled with fraud and corruption, despite being supervised by the UN – did not help; a coup for the Taliban. A re-run of the elections which was due to be held in November 2009 was cancelled indefinitely, as the only other major challenger to President Karzai, Doctor Abdullah Abdullah, withdrew his nomination. This means that by default President Karzai is still Afghanistan's President. President Karzai barely got half the votes cast during the election and even these figures are suspect.

The West will probably never succeed in cleaning up Afghan politics as corruption is part of daily life, a cultural norm. But at least the Afghan people had the chance to vote for somebody of their own choosing, a step in the right direction that most Afghans would appreciate.

NATO is doing a pretty good job under the circumstances in trying to get the Afghan National Army and Afghan National Police up to a standard where

Opposite:

F18s on over watch duty.

Morale in this Gurkha platoon certainly seems sky high.

Clockwise from top left:

British troops moving forward
during Op Aabi Toorah.

Explosives search dog hard at work.
In late 2009 an Australian one was
lost during an ambush, only to be
found later alive and well.

50 Cal HMG gunner on guard.

British troops on patrol in an alien
looking environment.

Clockwise from top left:

Brits cautiously advance following an IED incident.

In a scene reminiscent of WW1, British troops advance across a makeshift walk way.

British troops clear a compound during Op Diesel.

Mine and IED clearing British style.

Riding shotgun for a convoy is not the easiest job as you constantly have to be on the lookout for IEDs.

Scanning for Taliban activity during Op Diesel.

Vikings move forward in support of a British advance during Op Aabi Toorah.

they can take over the role of security – but that is going to take time. Once that day eventually comes around, the West can of course quit. But no one can have high expectations of instant prosperity or peace, at least not in the way those in the West would define it. Which leaves the Western powers with their moral obligation to the Afghan people – they promised them a better life.

From a security point of view, and despite their best efforts, they have largely failed them in this. Many of them are now being killed by IEDs left for ISAF. Many have been displaced during the fighting and they cannot go back to their homes for fear of being killed in the cross-fire. But morally the West has not failed everywhere, there are many examples of foreign presence helping the Afghans, such as in schooling, medical care, rights for women, local employment, and in the supply of electricity. One particular example of good work in Afghanistan concerns the birth of children in remote areas. At one time, as many as 50 women a year would lose their lives just because of a lack of trained medical personnel. Now, thanks to the efforts of a British charity able to work in these regions at last, the mortality rate amongst pregnant women has plummeted. The majority of Afghans have nothing personally against westerners in their country – indeed for the most part they are made to feel welcome – it is only those that they perceive to have hidden agendas that the Afghans mistrust.

Fortified Villages

At the time of writing the Taliban are throwing everything at NATO before the onset of winter. Perhaps NATO should revisit a concept that the British developed to defeat the communists in Malaya during the uprising there in the 1950s – and update it. This is the fortified village concept. This would call for tribes in the rural areas of Afghanistan in unison to seal themselves off from the Taliban – both physically and psychologically – denying them the ability to attack or intimidate their people. The idea is not foreign to the Afghans, there are many remote villages and farms that have large mud walls built around them for protection, usually from rival tribes, or raiders – but why not the Taliban?

Afghanistan is not Vietnam – and I mention this country because they tried the concept there after being suitably impressed with its performance in Malaya, only it failed. There were many reasons for its failure in Vietnam, including poor implementation, lack of support and good old fashioned corruption. In Vietnam they called it the Strategic Hamlet Program, a concept designed to provide the vulnerable population with security, social support and aid providing that they were willing to be resettled within a protected

Inset, clockwise from right:

British medics treat a wounded Afghan child.

British troops blow a mouse hole at the height
of Op Diesel.

All weapon systems require constant cleaning in
the dusty conditions of the Afghan desert.

US Marine taking stock of his route, looking out for ambush points and combat indicators.

Clockwise from top left:

Royal Marine laying down fire courtesy of a 51mm mortar.

Royal Marines advance across a waterway in southern Helmand.

An infantry soldier from New Zealand feeding a baby.

The Taliban flag.

An RAF Regiment combat tour t shirt logo.

An Operation Herrick t-shirt sold in aid of the Help for Heroes charity. Such items often end up on Ebay as a means of raising money for our wounded soldiers.

Royal Marines enjoy a game of rugby during a rare period of downtime.

village. Initially the Americans followed the British example and reshaped the villages to make them easier to protect. Any building outside the perimeter of these villages was destroyed to deny their use to enemy forces. To avoid the villagers within them feeling isolated, a network was set up that gave them the feeling of mutual protection. Also every man in the village was given a weapon and trained in its use.

The Strategic Hamlet Program then followed the British idea of clearing an area of insurgents first. Once this was done, a fortified village would be set up, and when completed the same principle would be applied to a nearby area, and then another, and so on until a network started to develop that provided a protective screen. This was called the 'ink spot' principle.

The British model, in addition to providing protection, also set out to improve the villagers' lives economically, politically, socially and culturally. The relationship between the government and the people would be strengthened. Such a concept could work in Afghanistan – as long as the above principles are applied. This would deny the Taliban both the means of intimidating the Afghan people and attacking ISAF forces. In addition, a Quick Reaction Force (QRF) – either Afghan or ISAF – could be put on permanent standby to assist in the event of an attack. One group of ISAF soldiers that would be excellent for such a role are the British Gurkhas, as the Afghans have immense respect for them. Their features are similar to the Afghans, and their Dari language can be understood by them.

Another idea worth pursuing in Afghanistan as part of such a strategy is the reintroduction of a light COIN (counter insurgency) type aircraft such as the Tucano. Being of a non-aggressive appearance, these aircraft have the ability to fly over a set area for hours on end without intimidating the locals. But should the need arise for close air support – they pack a very heavy punch. And by sheer coincidence, the UK has a number of these highly capable aircraft sitting in storage doing nothing. With a small number of modifications these could be brought into service very quickly at a fraction of the operating cost of a close support jet aircraft. A Tucano costs $1,000 per hour to operate, an F-15 costs $45,000. The soldiers at the front could certainly do with such an aircraft.

All of this is of course wishful thinking, but new ideas for Afghanistan's future must be raised and discussed to make sure that we have not overlooked any viable option. With respect to the fortified village concept, it is important to remember that although it failed in Vietnam, it was extremely successful in Malaya. Maybe it is time to take a good look at this concept once again. After all, what have we got to lose?

DENNIS ARMY AIRFIELD
ORGUN-E AFG Elev, 7460FT

DEDICATED TO THE OF PFC JEROD R.DENNIS
UNIT 3/504 SHK1N, AFG

Clockwise from left:

A US Tactical Air Control Party pose for a photo following a series of long and demanding missions in and around southern Afghanistan.

Royal Marines rest following a major operation in Helmand.

A British Para makes good use of a quad bike in Zabol Province; it's better than walking.

Quad bikes have proved invaluable in Afghanistan, as they can go down tracks that are impassable for a normal vehicle.

A British sniper cautiously advances through a poppy field, no doubt mindful of the ever-present IED threat.

The dune-buggy like Springer is the latest vehicle to be deployed to Afghanistan for helicopter and FOB support.

Below, main picture USMC Cobra providing fire support to ground forces after a contact.

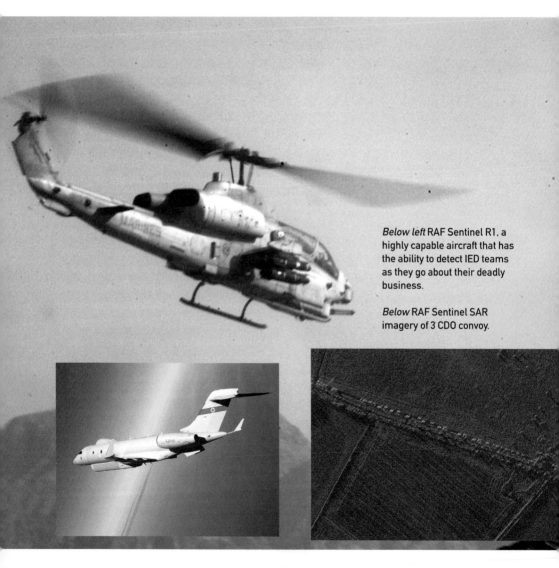

Below left RAF Sentinel R1, a highly capable aircraft that has the ability to detect IED teams as they go about their deadly business.

Below RAF Sentinel SAR imagery of 3 CDO convoy.

IX

COMBAT SITREP

2009 was one of the bloodiest years yet in Afghanistan's recent turbulent history, with no sign of any let-up in the intense fighting that passes for daily life. And British forces have been in the thick of it. This chapter is devoted to the brave men and women serving in Afghanistan as part of Operation Herrick. These are their stories – as told by them.

Numerous British military units were involved in Operation Panther's Claw and here are the diaries of some of the Commanding Officers of the main battle groups. The operation saw 3,000 British troops involved in the five-week operation, which started on 20 June 2009 with a helicopter assault into the Babaji area by The Black Watch, 3rd Battalion The Royal Regiment of Scotland (3 SCOTS), Battle Group. Their Commanding Officer (CO) tells their story here.

The operation's story is taken up by the CO of Battle Group (Centre South), the CO of the Danish Battle Group, The Light Dragoons' CO, the 2nd Battalion The Royal Welsh CO decribes their involvement in the operation, and the 3 SCOTS CO writes about the operation's conclusion.

Lieutenant Colonel Stephen Cartwright, Commanding Officer 3 SCOTS Battle Group

20 June 2009, The First Air Assault into a Key Drugs Bazaar

The Battle Group was privileged to be given the task of breaking into the Babaji area at the start of Operation PANTHER'S CLAW. We knew the enemy had laid an IED screen to the north of the area so I decided to launch an audacious air assault of two aviation strike companies behind the insurgent forward defences.

To achieve tactical surprise, the Battle Group used ten Chinook helicopters and inserted 350 men at 3.30am on 20 June in one wave. It was very successful

Main picture: US Marines on foot patrol in Helmand.

Below: USMC Cobra attack helicopter. Old but still highly effective.

A US Army Apache rides shotgun for a British convoy bound for Kajaki. Such protection is vital, as it minimises the risk of surprise attacks at vulnerable choke points.

Clockwise from top left:

Scots burning illegal uniforms found during a raid on Lakari Bazaar in Helmand.

The Hilton it certainly isn't, but FOB Inkerman it is. Home of 2 Para's mortar platoon.

A female Merlin pilot on work-up training in California prior to deployment to Afghanistan.

A battle-weary British soldier after a tiring day in Helmand.

and we had occupied defensive positions of our own by first light. The remainder of the Battle Group, in armoured and wheeled vehicles, approached from the north to link up. However, the enemy were watching us and began their assaults from 7am targeting our positions with a mixture of small arms fire and rocket- propelled grenades.

These initial attacks delayed our link-up but we consolidated our positions and defeated the enemy with our ability to overmatch their weapon systems. Our snipers were particularly effective in these early hours, although we did require support from guided rockets and attack helicopters. B Company to the west secured the compounds that dominated the wadi crossing and A Company to the east cleared the drugs bazaar of 15 IEDs whilst under harassing fire.

It was during this operation that an ANA [Afghan National Army] soldier, Wahid, was tragically killed by an IED as the company cleared to the extremities of the bazaar. Lance Corporal Stacey Quinn, a medic, was first on the scene, but despite her best efforts he died shortly after the explosion. Despite this setback, we successfully brought in our armoured vehicles, our logistics and the engineer equipment required to build the force protection. The aviation assault was supported by fast air, command helicopters and UAVs and given its complexity was an overwhelming tactical success.

For the next four days we consolidated our bridgehead into the insurgent-held territory and pushed them further to the south. The Royal Engineers built a protective 'Hesco' bastion wall across the wadi to control the population and to prevent the insurgents from escaping to the north. It was quickly nicknamed 'Hadrian's Wall'. B Company began to establish their operating base by building up the fortifications. Sporadic attacks continued every day and although we were in a defensive posture, the companies pushed forward with aggressive patrols to afford us the initiative that is so vital for a defensive battle.

On the second night, up to 30 insurgents assaulted A Company in the bazaar but were beaten back after a two-hour engagement. A conservative estimate would suggest that over half of their force was killed in this engagement alone. C Company, in their Jackal vehicles, pushed to the west and seized the top of the Shamalan canal in preparation for the link-up with the Welsh Guards. They too had to deal with a determined and persistent enemy who realised that they were losing their dominance of the area.

After the engineer work had been completed, the majority of the Battle Group extracted to [Camp] Bastion, leaving B Company to cover the whole area with their 180 personnel. They dominated the area, constantly keeping the enemy on the back foot and won every engagement. More importantly they starting engaging with the local nationals to the north of the wadi and established positive dialogue with the aim of getting them to return to their

Top left: USMC Husky IED clearance vehicles getting ready to clear an MSR prior to the arrival of a convoy.

Top right: US Marine with minimi 5.56mm SAW.

Above: British WMIKs clearing a possible ambush point.

Above left: Another hot day in Helmand.

Near left: British WMIK on convoy protection duty.

Left: US Marine taking cover after a contact report.

homes as soon as the fighting had ceased. Our contribution ended when B Company handed over the area to No 2 Company Welsh Guards on 4 July.

Lieutenant Colonel Doug Chalmers, Commanding Officer Battle Group (Centre South)

Our battalion has responsibility for Battle Group (Centre South) which means we are responsible for the districts of Nad e-Ali and Lashkar Gah. HERRICK 10 has seen the area under the Government of Afghanistan's control within these districts grow considerably.

Very early on in the tour a large ANA-led operation pushed the insurgents out of a town called Basharan and then kept them out. After a couple of days of fierce fighting the village was secured and has gone from strength to strength ever since. There is an increasing air of confidence in the village as they regain a sense of normality.

Within Nad e-Ali district centre the bazaar has continued to grow, with new shops opening every month. The residents, although still wary, have gained a degree of confidence in their future. They now believe us when we say that we are here to stay. Outside of the district centre there is insurgent activity but it is being mitigated by joint ANA, ANP [Afghan National Police] and ISAF [International Security Assistance Force] patrols. The fact that the farmers continue to work their fields and deliver a considerable amount of produce that includes vegetables and melons, indicates that they too have sufficient confidence to stay and work their land.

Less than a month ago in one of the opening moves of Operation PANTHER'S CLAW the ANP, assisted by the Prince of Wales's Company, moved rapidly north and secured the town of Chah-e Anjir. This is a large town that had effectively been under siege for over a year. The population is slowly gaining in confidence and we are starting to see the number of shops increase along with the variety of items for sale. It is early days but in several months it is likely to be at the same stage as the district centre is today.

More recently the Battle Group fought up the Shamalan canal to secure key crossings and prevent more insurgents flowing into the Babiji area. This has worked, and at the moment the farmers that work around these checkpoints have returned to their fields and started to interact with the ANA and ISAF soldiers on the canal.

These significant gains have been secured at a high cost in terms of lives and injuries to the Battle Group. But the sense of achievement is palpable and this does make the sacrifices easier to bear. We are now focused on deepening the confidence of the local residents in the areas that we have secured. They deserve a chance and we are giving it to them.

Colonel Frank Lissner,
Commanding Officer of the Danish Battle Group

Nahr-e-Burgha Canal – 2 and 8 July

Our role in Operation PANCHAI PALANG was to seize two of the crossing points along the Nahr-e-Burgha to allow The Light Dragoons Battle Group to enter an area which was under the de facto control of the insurgents.

Prior to PANCHAI PALANG, the insurgents in the region have skilfully and determinedly resisted any attempt by the Danish Battle Group to patrol in the area; both through fierce fighting and extensive use of improvised explosive devices, blocking all access points into the area. It had become a safe haven for the insurgents from where they launched attacks on both local Afghan National Security Forces [ANSF] checkpoints and objectives in Gereshk.

Soldiers from Battle Group Centre have, for the last year, both risked and lost lives patrolling in and around the operations area, and the Battle Group therefore very much welcomes the developments on the ground brought about by PANCHAI PALANG. This operation could indeed turn out to be the beginning of the end for the insurgents in central Helmand.

Following the cessation of fighting in the northern areas, most of the local population has now returned to their homes and have welcomed the ISAF forces in the area. Our task is now to assure enduring security within the area assisted by ANSF, local key leaders and the population.

Lieutenant Colonel Gus Fair,
Commanding Officer The Light Dragoons

The Sweep Across Spin Masjed & Babiji – 4 to 8 July and 10 to 14 July 2009

The clearance of Malgir and Babaji was one of the final phases of Op PANCHAI PALANG and was very much dependent on the hard work put in across the rest of the brigade. Having effectively sealed off the Green Zone, with the Welsh Guards blocking the west, the Danes the north and the east, and A Squadron of Light Dragoons the south, The Light Dragoons Battle Group was tasked to clear the Green Zone of Taliban and free the local people from their intimidation and brutality.

This we have done. The Battle Group broke in through a bridgehead secured by the Danish Battle Group and fought its way south through determined enemy resistance. We subsequently cleared our way west, and have now cleared the enemy from Malgir and Babaji.

This was the most intense fighting over a protracted period I have experienced in my 20 years in the Army. The men, women and equipment delivered

Clockwise from above:

Soldiers from 42 Commando board a Chinook after an operation in Helmand.

42 CDO move to clear the next set of compounds during Operation Diesel.

B Company Black Watch taking 5 after a long patrol.

An RAF Chinook kicks up dust after loading up cargo near a British supply convoy.

Soldiers from the Black Watch advance through a field. The IED menace means it feels slightly more comfortable to be at the back than at the front of the file.

Clockwise from left:

British forces on the move to a new FOB.

Australian gunners pose for a photo after helping their British mates out during a routine combined operation.

Chinook near Kandahar.

Black Watch provost Sgt taking a break. Walking around in heavy armour is extremely tiring work, so who can blame him.

A British soldier taking a cheeky peak through a mouse hole that his unit probably created during an earlier visit. Creating such holes is now standard practice as it helps soldiers avoid booby traps that have been laid in likely places.

more than we had any right to expect. The conditions could barely have been more testing and I am humbled by the extraordinary bravery, determination and resilience that I witnessed from soldiers ranging from the young female medic who walked every inch of the way to the 49-year-old TA WO2 [Territorial Army Warrant Officer Class 2] who ran a sniper team.

As a result of this operation many more Afghans are now living under the control of the Government of the Islamic Republic of Afghanistan; people who were previously subject to the rule of the Taliban. They can now live without the fear of the Taliban visiting in the middle of the night; they have the freedom to vote in next month's elections; the chance to look forward to enjoying some of the rights and privileges that we are lucky enough to take for granted.

Progress such as this does not come for free, and we have paid a heavy price. The fierce fighting resulted in the deaths of Private Laws 2 MERCIAN [2nd Battalion The Mercian Regiment (Worcesters & Foresters)], Lance Corporal Elson 1st Battalion Welsh Guards, and Lance Corporal Dennis and Trooper Whiteside from The Light Dragoons. Four Afghan soldiers have also lost their lives fighting alongside us, and their commitment and dedication to their country's future should not be underestimated. The cost on the enemy should also not go unreported; we have comprehensively defeated the Taliban wherever we have found him, and his losses have been far in excess of ours.

Some will ask whether the progress is worth the cost. I can answer for everyone in my Battle Group when I answer with a resounding 'yes'. At the beginning of this tour, the Battle Group deployed to Garmsir, now under command of the US Marines. Many of the soldiers had fought there in 2007 as we battled the Taliban for control of the district centre. The progress we saw there was remarkable. Where we had once fought in a deserted and ruined town, there is now a burgeoning market and people are able to go about their day-to-day lives in peace. Wheat was being grown instead of poppy, and the people were able to determine their own future independent of either ISAF or Taliban control.

That progress is achievable in Babaji and Malgir, and already we are seeing people attending shuras with both ISAF and the local governance. However, the Taliban recognise the threat, and progress will not come without the continued efforts of the soldiers under my command and those that replace them. Some of them will give up their lives to achieve this, as will some Afghans we fight alongside, but we know that we owe it to those killed and injured over the last month, the people who we have liberated with the promise of a better life, and the people in the UK whose way of life we seek to defend, to ensure that we do not fail.

Major Nigel Crewe-Read,
Officer Commanding C Company, 2nd Battalion The Royal Welsh

The Armoured Thrust Through Babiji – 20 to 25 July 2009

Accompanied by artillery from 52 (Niagara) Battery Royal Artillery, engineers from 11 Field Squadron Royal Engineers, IED clearance teams, and military-civilian reconstruction teams, we conducted a swift night move from Bastion to Forward Operating Base Price. As dawn came the company was escorted down through the areas that had been liberated from the Taliban. It was obvious that there had been quite a fight to achieve the earlier goals of PANTHER'S CLAW.

Crossing the line of departure, everyone was braced for what could be a very bloody fight. Breaking off the main track to avoid IEDs, the Warriors began to move into the Helmand Green Zone. This was the first time Warriors had ever actually been taken into the complex terrain of the Green Zone which consists of many irrigation ditches, flooded fields, and sprawling compounds. Not easy terrain for 36 tonnes of armour to cross without becoming stuck. The lead platoon scouted a route ahead with the rest of the company following behind. Engineer support was integral to the company and proved useful in fording many of the ditches. Combat aircraft, unmanned aerial vehicles and attack helicopters co-ordinated by the artillery provided air cover and overwatch as the company swept forward.

The first objective, the village of Tabella, was reached at mid-day and the company formed up into assault formation. The time for the assault came and the Warriors surged forward across the open bazaar onto the objective. Meeting no enemy resistance, we dismounted from our vehicles and began to sweep through the village to check it was clear of insurgents. Conducting a thorough clearance took time, but by 1700 the village was deemed to be clear of insurgents. A local shura was then conducted with local Afghans to reassure them of ISAF's good intentions and that ISAF would remain in the area to provide security for them.

At 0600 on the second day, 21 July, the clearance of the next village, Bahloy Kalay, started. This was an even bigger objective to clear than the previous village. Three platoons were tasked with this, and they made good progress through the intense heat of the Afghan day. Local Afghans greeted us and proved very friendly, offering us refreshments as well as passing us information and even lending a helping hand to repair a broken-down Warrior. By evening the village was clear of enemy fighters and a further 92 compounds had been cleared. Again, a shura was held at 1630 to reassure locals of ISAF intentions.

At 0530 on 22 July, the company handed over the secured villages to The Light Dragoons Battle Group and moved to clear a route from those villages up to the Welsh Guards Battle Group in the north west. The company moved

Clockwise from right:

British forces leaving for Mirabat.

British female drivers at FOB Nolay.

British convoy on the move to FOB Nolay.

A Gurkha preparing to move out on patrol.

down to a vast cemetery and then turned north to clear the route. Progress was measured as the company moved forward with dismounted patrols providing flank security, the IED clearance team working flat out, engineers providing essential support to cross large irrigation ditches, and the artillery co-ordinating the air cover. After a day of hard work the company paused overnight in a defensive position and then moved forward again at 0500 on 23 July. Progress continued to be made, and by 1800 the company had reached the Welsh Guards Battle Group, linking the two Battle Groups together.

Overall, although the operation had not involved any fighting, it was a great success. Locals stated that the Taliban had run away as soon as they saw the Warriors coming. A total of 198 compounds had been secured, 12km of Green Zone had been crossed in heavy armoured vehicles, and the area had been cleared of armed Taliban fighters, allowing the Government of Afghanistan's influence to begin in this area which had once been the heartland of insurgent resistance.

Lieutenant Colonel Stephen Cartwright, Commanding Officer 3 SCOTS

The Final Air Assault Linked with the Armoured Thrust – 20 to 27 July 2009

It seemed apt that, having been involved at the very start of the British strike in Babaji, we should be allowed to take part in its finale. Once again, we were given enough Chinooks to lift the aviation element of the Battle Group in a single wave. As with our first Battle Group operation, the key lay in surprising the insurgents.

The Battle Group for this operation consisted of Alpha (Grenadier) Company, 3 SCOTS; C Company, 2 R WELSH [2nd Battalion The Royal Welsh] mounted in Warrior fighting vehicles [their role mentioned above]; and Assaye Squadron, Light Dragoons, in armoured recce vehicles; 500 personnel and 60 vehicles. A Company swooped on the target area by Chinook, Charlie Company led an armoured punch in through the Green Zone (the first of its kind) from the east using Warrior armoured fighting vehicles. They were joined by Assaye Squadron. Our logistics tail followed up in Mastiff troop carriers and armoured trucks.

It became immediately clear that the brigade plan had been a huge success. The isolation of the area and the success of The Light Dragoons Battle Group's battle in the north east had taken its toll against the insurgents. Both the aviation assault and armoured manoeuvre avoided the expected IED screen and the remaining insurgents realised that they were completely overmatched by the combat power and melted into the Green Zone. The local population was initially cautious but slowly they realised that ISAF intended to stay in the area for good and became very helpful. In turn, we provided our doctor to start conducting medical clinics. The Light Dragoons even organised a football afternoon which attracted 30 youngsters.

Further to the west in our operational area, A Company was dominating the insurgents' old ground. Shuras were arranged quickly and the relationships are developing well. The insurgents mounted a lame attack on the night of 24 July but they were quickly overwhelmed by A Company. C Company did a fantastic job of clearing a supply route north, linking us up to the Luy Mandah wadi that the Battle Group seized at the start of the operation. They found several IEDs laid waiting for them, which their attached bomb disposal officers destroyed in situ.

Tragically, our luck ran out on 25 July when my Fire Support Group, who had re-inserted into the area in Jackal vehicles, hit an IED. One soldier was killed and several others wounded. Another IED also caused injuries. The Fire Support Group had been searching for potential polling station locations for the presidential elections, underlining the stark contrast between the aims of the Battle Group and the insurgents' aims in the area. Throughout the next 48 hours it became clear that there were insurgent IED teams operating in the area and several inadvertently killed themselves whilst laying devices. A Company continued to dominate the ground, understand the locals' concerns and kill insurgents, wherever they could find them. The Battle Group extracted by vehicle and Chinook early on 27 July.

It has been an immense operation; emotionally and physically exhausting but exhilarating at the same time. As the Regional Battle Group (South), I am delighted that 3 SCOTS have contributed so much to 19 Light Brigade's PANTHER'S CLAW. I am certain that everyone in the Battle Group will look back in a few years to an extraordinary operation when we did our jobs in the most demanding environment. The main factor of the success has been team work from the lowest infantry section to the whole brigade. I am very proud of my jocks, gunners, sappers, redcaps and signallers. Their contribution to the UK's summer offensive has been outstanding. The Battle Group's attention now turns to other operations in southern Afghanistan but we will never forget those that they gave their lives during this one.

Combat Report July 2009

A final armoured thrust across enemy territory has marked the end of Operation PANTHER'S CLAW; a five-week campaign to clear one of the few remaining Taliban strongholds in Helmand province.

Top to bottom:

Gurkha Kamal Thapa lets rip near Musa Qaleh.

A British WMIK blocks off a road prior to the arrival of a supply convoy.

British observation mouse hole near Musa Qalah.

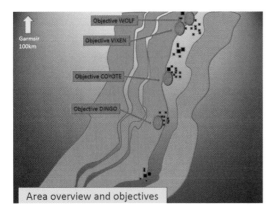

Area overview and objectives

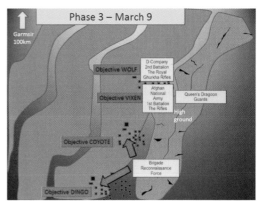

Phase 3 – March 9

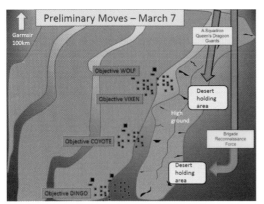

Preliminary Moves – March 7

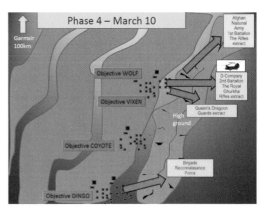

Phase 4 – March 10

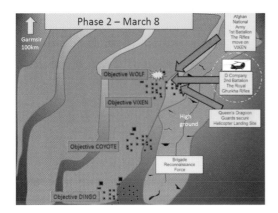

Phase 2 – March 8

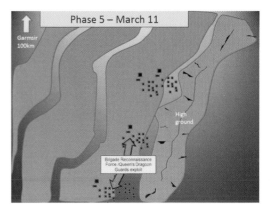

Phase 5 – March 11

Operation Kapcha Baz as it happened day by day, March 2009. Led by the Queen's Dragoon Guards, 250 British and 100 ANA soldiers hit Taliban targets on the banks of the river Helmand 1000km south of Garmsir. After fierce firefights the Taliban were routed and fled. Major Andy Watkins, OC C Company 1st Battalion The Rifles, commented: 'The operation was an excellent demonstration of how effective the ANA are becoming.'

The operation, known as PANCHAI PALANG in Pashtu, has cleared and secured the area between Lashkar Gah and Gereshk, a region which is home to up to 80,000 Helmandis. In a fiercely fought battle with the insurgents, British forces inflicted heavy losses on enemy forces, severely damaging their command and control structures and visibly weakening their resistance. As the fighting subsided and insurgents fled from their hidden positions, local people started to flock back to the previously deserted towns and villages. The final push in the five-week-long operation began in the early hours of 20 July 2009 when a mechanised Warrior company from 2nd Battalion The Royal Welsh (2 Royal Welsh) pushed south west from Spin Masjed in an armoured sweep towards the east bank of the Luy Mandah wadi. Simultaneously, four Chinooks carrying 160 men from The Black Watch, 3rd Battalion The Royal Regiment of Scotland (3 SCOTS), swooped into the Green Zone to secure nearby key ground in the west of Babiji. One hundred and forty men from 2 Royal Welsh in a convoy of Warriors, supported by tanks from a Danish battalion, pushed through the lush green countryside in the heart of the Green Zone, while their Scottish colleagues used the element of surprise to storm across land just a short distance away.

The Royal Welsh cut through the countryside to avoid potentially lethal tracks and roadways strewn with improvised explosive devices (IEDs), linking up with 3 SCOTS who had pushed along the Babiji Road. The battle groups encountered relatively little resistance, an indication that Taliban fighters have fled the area as their hierarchy has fallen apart following the sustained attack over the past five weeks. Lieutenant Colonel Nick Richardson, spokesman for Task Force Helmand, said:

We have encountered very few insurgents on the last leg of Operation PANCHAI PALANG. This is a very positive sign. Rather than being attacked at every turn, as we saw when The Light Dragoons first entered Spin Masjed, the battle groups received a welcome from the locals, many of whom openly expressed how pleased they are to see the demise of Taliban influence in the area.

Operation PANTHER'S CLAW began on 19 June 2009 when 350 soldiers from 3 SCOTS conducted a high risk air assault securing a canal crossing and a key Taliban drugs bazaar on the Nahr-e-Burgha. This was followed by a push up the Shamalan canal by the 1st Battalion Welsh Guards, who secured 14 crossings, either establishing checkpoints or blocking them to create a barrier to movement and cutting off the insurgents' supply route. Nearer Gereshk, in a co-ordinated move, the Danish Battle Group left Forward Operating Base Price in armoured vehicles with the mission of securing two other crossing points along the Nahr-e-Burgha canal to allow The Light Dragoons Battle

Group to move deep into the enemy territory of Spin Masjed. Initially, The Light Dragoons encountered fierce fighting through compounds in sweltering heat which at times baked the earth to a temperature which prevented them from lying prone on the ground in the face of enemy fire.

Battle Group continued to make progress across the area, securing compounds one by one, often battling through prolonged enemy fire. As they broke through the crust of enemy defences they found 55 dug-in IEDs, had 53 small arms and rocket-propelled grenade engagements and also faced a series of complex ambushes. The Battle Group sustained their own losses but the losses of the insurgents were much, much greater. Five days into the fight enemy resistance began to weaken as their command and control was decimated by the resilience of British and Afghan forces. The Afghan National Army, mentored by 2nd Battalion The Mercian Regiment, played a key part in the operation, searching compounds and assisting the Afghan National Police with manning the recently captured crossing points. As The Light Dragoons moved across the 'Panther's Claw Triangle', the insurgents were pushed further and further towards the Shamalan canal. On 10 July 2009, 3 SCOTS inserted 160 men on four Chinooks into the Babiji region, with the intention that they would clear another patch of land and expand their area of control to meet with The Light Dragoons Battle Group, who were still working their way down from Spin Masjed. Within hours of landing in enemy territory, the Scottish regiment found a large narcotics lab probably used to fund the insurgents' activities. A massive quantity of precursor chemicals and 5kg of a morphine-derivative substance that was one step away from becoming heroin were destroyed in situ by the Afghan Counter Narcotics Police. After 3 SCOTS had successfully linked up with The Light Dragoons, they combined and doubled their effort to drive deeper into the area. They began to see a subtle change in atmospherics with the local population welcoming the soldiers and willingly pointing out cleared routes and IEDs that they knew to be dug into the ground.

The final air assault began the last phase of the operation, combined with an armoured thrust to clear any remaining Taliban fighters still loitering in the area in small numbers. Three thousand soldiers were involved in Operation PANTHER'S CLAW, with Afghan, Danish, Estonian and US contingents playing a crucial role. Together they have successfully cleared an area the size of the Isle of Wight; a region which had previously been under complete Taliban influence from where they had launched repeated attacks with relative impunity.

Brigadier Tim Radford, Commander Task Force Helmand, said:

> Our intention with this operation was, in the short term, to clear the area in advance of the presidential and provincial elections so that we could ensure

Clockwise from top left:

A British soldier giving a mate a helping hand up a steep bank.

British troops embark on Op Aabi Toorah.

British troops go through the mouse hole during Op Diesel.

Jackals on the prowl in Helmand.

British GPMG gunner on Operation Aabi Toorah.

British supply convoy on the move during Op Diesel.

Clockwise from left:

A British GPMG gunner keeps a vigilant watch during Op Diesel.

A British Army officer gives a sitrep at the height of Op Panthers Claw.

Private Leon Wilson – maybe the luckiest man in the British Army – showing off the helmet that saved his life from a Taliban bullet.

British forces on the move during Op Panther's Claw.

An RAF Chinook kicks up dust during a troop insertion at the height of Operation Panther's Claw.

that the Afghan people were free to exercise their democratic rights. In the longer term, it was to remove the insurgents and hold the region, alongside Afghan forces, to allow reconstruction and development to take place. What we have achieved here is significant and I am absolutely certain that the operation has been a success. But I want to be clear about what that success means. It means that we have hit hard at the heart of the insurgency and we have weakened their structures and command.

But I am aware that the effort in Helmand still has a long way to go. We have inflicted heavy losses on the insurgents, both physically and psychologically, and we have seen a number of them give up and flee the area as a result. But there will be some that simply melt back into the local population and so, for us, the threat continues to bubble beneath the surface.

Over time, we must build on what has already been achieved to eliminate the threat completely and that will take time. Providing the lasting security for reconstruction and development to take place in this region is now key to a future free from the insurgents' influence. We are beginning to see local people return and they are pleased that the insurgents have been driven out. I am immensely proud of what my soldiers have achieved and I remain cautiously optimistic about the future. Tragically, during PANTHER'S CLAW nine brave young men paid the ultimate sacrifice. We are a close knit Task Force and we all feel those losses very deeply but we remain resolute and determined to continue the fight in their name.

This operation has been the focus of an enormous amount of media attention for various reasons. But sometimes obscured by the wider political debates are a group of men and women doing a truly extraordinary job. Out on the ground I have seen for myself the selfless bravery and commitment that they are displaying each and every day. It is something that the British public should be justifiably proud of.

Combat Report August 2009

British and Afghan forces destroy Taliban compounds and opium processing facilities in the Sangin Valley, Afghanistan.

Operation TYRUNA saw 18 UK, US and Australian helicopters carrying 300 soldiers from The Black Watch, 3rd Battalion The Royal Regiment of Scotland, accompanied by Afghan National Army troops, descended on the Taliban stronghold of Malmand Chinah, close to Ghowrak in the Sangin Valley, just after nightfall on 7 August 2009. Nine Chinooks, three Black Hawks, two Sea Kings and four Apache attack helicopters swept across a vast expanse of open desert before targeting the remote and isolated compound area to clear it of suspected Taliban fighters. After the initial air assault hundreds of soldiers filed off the helicopters before moving into the heart of Malmand Chinah.

The British and Afghan troops were soon engaged by Taliban fighters lying in wait for them. The troops returned fire and were drawn into a short but fierce fight through the rabbit warren of rooms in the mud compounds. They then mounted a fierce attack with explosives experts smashing their way through the Taliban-ridden compounds by blasting holes in the walls to allow a stream of soldiers to flood into the area, sweeping through one narcotics lab after another.

Using sniffer dogs they pinpointed and seized a massive haul of 250 kilograms of wet opium as well as a number of weapons, all of which was destroyed in situ. By the break of dawn, the troops extracted from the compounds to the makeshift helicopter landing site in the desert, where a fleet of helicopters reloaded the troops and took them back to their base in Kandahar. It is thought that seven insurgents were killed during the assault.

Major Robin Lindsay from The Black Watch, 3rd Battalion The Royal Regiment of Scotland, led the operation.

> This was a highly successful operation. This type of high intensity technique, where we airlift a large number of troops into a small area, effectively storming it, has been shown to work time after time.
>
> It proves to the Taliban beyond doubt that they have no safe havens even in the most remote, isolated places. We can hit them at will wherever and whoever they are. There are no out-of-bounds areas for ISAF troops.
>
> The money that would have come from the sale of the opium would undoubtedly have funded the insurgents' activities, further strengthening their hold in the area and their ability to launch deadly attacks on coalition forces. This kind of operation hits at the heart of the insurgency because it significantly reduces their capability to continue the fight. With fewer numbers and diminished resources, they are simply less effective.

Soldiers from The Black Watch, 3rd Battalion The Royal Regiment of Scotland, lay down covering fire during the operation in Malmand Chinah in the Sangin Valley, home to the forces of seven nationalities within the ISAF coalition, many of which worked together on this operation as well as local Afghan forces, the effectiveness of which Major Lindsay praised:

> This air assault highlights the truly multi-national nature of operations in Afghanistan. Notably, we were accompanied by quite a number of our Afghan counterparts and the success of the operation is also testament to their effectiveness. They are committed, professional and brave; a true force to be reckoned with.

Above: A Royal Marine scopes out a target during Op Aabi Toorah ('Blue Sword'). One of the key objectives of the op was to attack the Taliban stronghold of Marjah, to show that ISAF could operate when and where it chose, in this case a Taliban heartland.

Top right: Royal Marines clearing a compound near the Kajaki dam.

Middle right: A Welsh guard spots Taliban moving in his location.

Right: Royal Marines enter an abandoned village in Helmand.

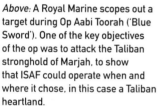

Clockwise from left:

A Royal Marine scopes out a possible target during Op Sond Chara.

Royal Marines cast their long shadows during Op Sond Chara.

A British NCO barks out some orders during a clearance operation. Note the fixed bayonet.

Welsh Guards exiting a US Black Hawk on Op Panchai Palang 2.

Soldiers from the Royal Welsh Regiment speed past a group of Afghans during Op Panther's Claw.

The battalion took over as the Regional Battle Group (South) on 10 April 2009. 3 SCOTS are part of 19 Light Brigade who currently make up Task Force Helmand but 3 SCOTS are responsible for supporting a variety of operations across the whole of southern Afghanistan, not just those of the main UK Task Force in Helmand province.

Combat Report October 2009

Soldiers from Alpha (Grenadier) Company of The Black Watch, 3rd Battalion The Royal Regiment of Scotland (3 SCOTS), have fought off Taliban attackers in order to facilitate the recovery of a US Army Chinook helicopter. When the helicopter of the US 82nd Combat Aviation Brigade suffered a hard landing on difficult ground in the Upper Sangin Valley, troops from 3 SCOTS were mobilised at short notice to secure the crash site. A number of UK and Afghan troops had been on the troop-carrying aircraft but thankfully, although it was badly damaged, no-one was injured.

In a bid to secure the area, recover the airframe and to prevent it falling into Taliban hands, 120 men of Alpha (Grenadier) Company were flown to the desert site.

However, as a specialist US recovery team set to work to prepare the Chinook for extraction, insurgents began to mass.

Air cover was called in and devastating strikes by US attack helicopters and A-10 jets killed and injured several insurgents; one badly injured insurgent was subsequently treated by 3 SCOTS' medics and evacuated by helicopter to an International Security Assistance Force medical facility. This was sufficient to discourage the attackers and the rest of the day passed off without major incident.

With the crash site secured the helicopter was extracted just as the light began to fade; it was underslung beneath another helicopter and slowly lifted away to the safety of Kandahar Airfield.An hour later the men of Alpha Company followed on and returned back to base. Major Matt Munro, Officer Commanding Alpha (Grenadier) Company, said:

> I'm delighted that this operation went so well. Given that we have worked so closely with the American aviators of the 82nd Combat Aviation Brigade throughout our seven-month tour I'm pleased that we were able to play an important part in the recovery of one of their airframes. It was a team effort that highlighted our high levels of preparedness and combat-readiness.

Major Neil Kugler, Operations Officer of Task Force (TF) Tallon, 82nd Combat Aviation Brigade, said:

> The troopers of TF Tallon and the Jocks of The Black Watch, 3 SCOTS Battle Group, developed a great professional relationship over the past four months during the conduct of numerous combat air assault operations. It was fitting that the final combat mission in Afghanistan for The Black Watch was to recover one of our damaged aircraft.

Lance Corporal Aaron Graham, aged 20 from Kirkcaldy, and a Section Second-in-Command in 1 Platoon, said:

> This was unlike any other job we have done out here. Once again we produced the goods and were pleased to keep the Taliban firmly on the back foot.

Commander's Initial Assessment, General Stanley McChrystal

[This is a heavily edited version of General Stanley McChrystal's Commander's Initial Assessment of how things stood in 2009 in Afghanistan from ISAF's point of view. Are these still his beliefs in 2010?]

Contents
Military Plans
Command and Control, and Command Relationships
USG Integrated Civil-Military Campaign Plan
Strategic Communication
Afghan National Security Force (ANSF) Growth and Acceleration

The stakes in Afghanistan are high. NATO's Comprehensive Strategic Political Military Plan and President Obama's strategy to disrupt, dismantle, and eventually defeat al Qaeda and prevent their return to Afghanistan have laid out a clear path of what we must do.

Stability in Afghanistan is an imperative; if the Afghan government falls to the Taliban – or has insufficient capability to counter transnational terrorists – Afghanistan could again become a base for terrorism, with obvious implications for regional stability. The situation in Afghanistan is serious; neither success nor failure can be taken for granted. Although considerable effort and sacrifice have resulted in some progress, many indicators suggest the overall situation is deteriorating. We face not only a resilient and growing insurgency;

Canadian soldiers from 3 RCR advance forward under the protection of an ANA machine gunner.

there is also a crisis of confidence among Afghans – in both their government and the international community – that undermines our credibility and emboldens the insurgents.

Further, a perception that our resolve is uncertain makes Afghans reluctant to align with us against the insurgents. Success is achievable, but it will not be attained simply by trying harder or 'doubling down' on the previous strategy. Additional resources are required, but focusing on force or resource requirements misses the point entirely. NATO's International Security Assistance Force (ISAF) requires a new strategy that is credible to, and sustainable by, the Afghans. This new strategy must also be properly resourced and executed through an integrated civilian-military counterinsurgency campaign that earns the support of the Afghan people and provides them with a secure environment. To execute the strategy, we must grow and improve the effectiveness of the Afghan National Security Forces (ANSF) and elevate the importance of governance.

Redefining the Fight

This is a different kind of fight. We must conduct classic counterinsurgency operations in an environment that is uniquely complex. Three regional insurgencies have intersected with a dynamic blend of local power struggles in a country damaged by 30 years of conflict. This makes for a situation that defies simple solutions or quick fixes. Success demands a comprehensive counterinsurgency (COIN) campaign. Our strategy cannot be focused on seizing terrain or destroying insurgent forces; our objective must be the population. In the struggle to gain the support of the people, every action we take must enable this effort.

Many describe the conflict in Afghanistan as a war of ideas, which I believe to be true. However, this is a 'deeds-based' information environment where perceptions derive from actions, such as how we interact with the population and how quickly things improve. The key to changing perceptions lies in changing the underlying truths. We must never confuse the situation as it stands with the one we desire, lest we risk our credibility.

The fight is not an annual cyclical campaign of kinetics driven by an insurgent 'fighting season.' Rather, it is a year-round struggle, often conducted with little apparent violence, to win the support of the people. Protecting the population from insurgent coercion and intimidation demands a persistent presence and focus that cannot be interrupted without risking serious setback.

Second, and more importantly, we face both a short and long-term fight. The long-term fight will require patience and commitment, but I believe the short-term fight will be decisive. ISAF is a conventional force that is poorly configured for COIN, inexperienced in local languages and culture, and struggling with challenges inherent to coalition warfare. Pre-occupied with protection of our own forces, we have operated in a manner that distances us – physically and psychologically – from the people we seek to protect. In addition, we run the risk of strategic defeat by pursuing tactical wins that cause civilian casualties or unnecessary collateral damage. The insurgents cannot defeat us militarily; but we can defeat ourselves.

A Strategy for Success: Balancing Resources and Risk

Our campaign in Afghanistan has been historically under-resourced and remains so today. Almost every aspect of our collective effort and associated resourcing has lagged a growing insurgency – historically a recipe for failure in COIN. Success will require a discrete 'jump' to gain the initiative, demonstrate progress in the short term, and secure long-term support. Resources will not win this war, but under-resourcing could lose it.

Ideally, the ANSF must lead this fight, but they will not have enough capability in the near-term given the insurgency's growth rate. In the interim, coalition forces must provide a bridge capability to protect critical segments of the population.

Unique Moment in Time

This is an important – and likely decisive – period of this war. Afghans are frustrated and weary after eight years without evidence of the progress they anticipated. Patience is understandably short, both in Afghanistan and in our own countries. Time matters; we must act now to reverse the negative trends and demonstrate progress. I do not underestimate the enormous challenges in executing this new strategy; however, we have a key advantage: the majority of Afghans do not want a return of the Taliban.

Overall the situation is deteriorating despite considerable effort by ISAF. The threat has grown steadily but subtly, and unchecked by commensurate counter-action, its severity now surpasses the capabilities of the current strategy. We cannot succeed simply by trying harder; ISAF must now adopt a fundamentally new approach. First, ISAF must improve execution and the understanding of the basics of COIN – those essential elements common to any counterinsurgency strategy. Second, ISAF requires a new strategy to counter a growing threat. In particular, there are two fundamental elements where ISAF must improve: change the operational culture of ISAF to focus on protecting the Afghan people, understanding their environment, and building relationships with them, and; transform ISAF processes to be more operationally efficient and effective.

Clockwise from left:

US 82nd Airborne soldiers surround their vehicle convoy during a local meeting with Afghan elders.

A soldier from the mighty 82nd does his bit in the more benign aspect of the psy-ops battle; a moment of light relief during a long patrol.

US Airborne take cover, following a contact report – a local Afghan nearby seems unconcerned.

Soldiers from 82nd Airborne prepare to assault a Taliban compound.

Describing the Mission

ISAF's mission statement is: 'ISAF, in support of GIRoA [Government of the Islamic Republic of Afghanistan], conducts operations in Afghanistan to reduce the capability and will of the insurgency, support the growth in capacity and capability of the Afghan National Security Forces (ANSF), and facilitate improvements in governance and socio-economic development, in order to provide a secure environment for sustainable stability that is observable to the population.'

Nature of the Conflict

While not a war in the conventional sense, the conflict in Afghanistan demands a similar focus and an equal level of effort, and the consequences of failure are just as grave. The fight also demands an improved and evolved level of understanding. The conflict in Afghanistan is often described as a war of ideas and perceptions; this is true and demands important consideration.

Redefining the Fight

The conflict in Afghanistan can be viewed as a set of related insurgencies, each of which is a complex system with multiple actors and a vast set of interconnecting relationships among those actors. The most important implication of this view is that no element of the conflict can be viewed in isolation – a change anywhere will affect everything else. The new strategy redefines the nature of the fight. It is not a cyclical, kinetic campaign based on a set 'fighting season.' Rather it is a continuous, year-long effort to help GIRoA win the support of the people and counter insurgent coercion and intimidation.

ISAF's center of gravity is the will and ability to provide for the needs of the population 'by, with, and through' the Afghan government. A foreign army alone cannot beat an insurgency; the insurgency in Afghanistan requires an Afghan solution. ISAF and the international community must provide substantial assistance to Afghanistan until the Afghan people make the decision to support their government and are capable of providing for their own security.

All ethnicities, particularly the Pashtuns, have traditionally sought a degree of independence from the central government, particularly when it is not seen as acting in the best interests of the population. These and other factors result in elements of the population tolerating the insurgency and calling to push out foreigners. The complex social landscape of Afghanistan is in many ways much more difficult to understand than Afghanistan's enemies. Insurgent groups have been the focus of U.S. and allied intelligence for many years; however, ISAF has not sufficiently studied Afghanistan's peoples whose needs, identities and grievances vary from province to province and from valley to valley. This complex environment is challenging to understand, particularly for foreigners.

Finally, either side can succeed in this conflict: GIRoA by securing the support of the people and the insurgents by controlling them. While this multi-faceted model of the fight is centred on the people, it is not symmetrical: the insurgents can also succeed more simply by preventing GIRoA from achieving their goals before the international community becomes exhausted.

Insurgent Groups

Most insurgent fighters are Afghans. They are directed by a small number of Afghan senior leaders based in Pakistan that work through an alternative political infrastructure in Afghanistan. They are aided by foreign fighters, elements of some intelligence agencies, and international funding, resources, and training. Foreign fighters provide materiel, expertise, and ideological commitment. The insurgents wage a 'silent war' of fear, intimidation, and persuasion throughout the year – not just during the warmer weather 'fighting season' – to gain control over the population.

The major insurgent groups in order of their threat to the mission are: the Quetta Shura Taliban (QST), the Haqqani Network (HQN), and the Hezb-e-Islami Gulbuddin (HiG). These groups coordinate activities loosely, often achieving significant unity of purpose and even some unity of effort, but they do not share a formal command-and-control structure. They also do not have a single overarching strategy or campaign plan. Each individual group, however, has a specific strategy, develops annual plans, and allocates resources accordingly. Each group has its own methods of developing and executing these plans and each has adapted over time. Despite the best efforts of GIRoA and ISAF, the insurgents currently have the initiative.

Insurgent Strategy and Campaign Design

The insurgents have two primary objectives: controlling the Afghan people and breaking the coalition's will. Their aim is to expel international forces and influences and to supplant GIRoA. At the operational level, the Quetta Shura conducts a formal campaign review each winter, after which Mullah Omar announces his guidance and intent for the coming year. The QST has been working to control Kandahar and its approaches for several years and there are indications that their influence over the city and neighboring districts is significant and growing.

HQN aims to regain eventually full control of its traditional base in Khowst, Paktia, and Paktika. HQN controls some of the key terrain around Khowst and

Left to right: A US soldier makes a new friend while out on patrol, which is equally as important as fighting the Taliban as winning the hearts and minds of the Afghan people is key to winning the conflict.

Soldiers survey a distant valley following an arduous climb to gain a better eyes on.

An Australian soldier surveys a distant area looking for combat indicators.

can influence the population in the region. Gulbuddin Hekmatyar's HiG maintains militant bases in Nangarhar, Nuristan, and Kunar, as well as Pakistan, but he also sustains political connections through HiG networks and aims to negotiate a major role in a future Taliban government. He does not currently have geographical objectives as is the case with the other groups.

All three insurgent groups require resources – mainly money and manpower. The O5T derives funding from the narcotics trade and external donors. HQN similarly draws resources principally from Pakistan, Gulf Arab networks, and from its close association with al Qaeda and other Pakistan-based insurgent groups. HiG seeks control of mineral wealth and smuggling routes in the east. The O5T's main efforts focus on the governance line of operations. ISAF's tendency to measure the enemy predominantly by kinetic events masks the true extent of insurgent activity and prevents an accurate assessment of the insurgents' intentions, progress, and level of control of the population.

Governance

The QST [Quetta Shura Taliban] has a governing structure in Afghanistan under the rubric of the Islamic Emirate of Afghanistan. They appoint shadow governors for most provinces, review their performance, and replace them periodically. They established a body to receive complaints against their own 'officials' and to act on them.

Major insurgent groups use violence, coercion and intimidation against civilians to control the population. They seek to inflict casualties on ISAF forces to break the will of individual ISAF countries and the coalition as a whole. They also use military activities to shape ISAF actions by denying freedom of movement, denying access to the population, and defending important terrain. The insurgents use the psychological effects of IEDs and the coalition force's preoccupation with force protection to reinforce the garrison posture and mentality. The major insurgent groups target GIRoA and ANSF [Afghan National Security Forces] to dissuade cooperation with the government and to show that GIRoA is ineffective.

Criminal Networks

Criminality creates a pool of manpower, resources, and capabilities for insurgents and contributes to a pervasive sense of insecurity among the people. Extensive smuggling diverts major revenue from GIRoA.

Criminality exacerbates the fragmentation of Afghan society and increases its susceptibility to insurgent penetration. A number of Afghan Government officials, at all levels, are reported to be complicit in these activities, further undermining GIRoA credibility.

Narcotics and Financing

The most significant aspect of the production and sale of opium and other narcotics is the corrosive and destabilizing impact on corruption within GIRoA. Narcotics activity also funds insurgent groups, however the importance of this funding must be understood within the overall context of insurgent financing, some of which comes from other sources.

Insurgent Vulnerabilities

The insurgents have important and exploitable shortcomings; they are not invulnerable. Command and control frictions and divergent goals hamper insurgent planning and restrict coordination of operations. In summary, ISAF confronts a loose federation of insurgent groups that are sophisticated, organized, adaptive, determined, and nuanced across all lines of operations, with many enablers, but not without vulnerability. These groups are dangerous and, if not effectively countered, could exhaust the coalition and prevent GIRoA from being able to govern the state of Afghanistan.

The Afghan government has made progress, yet serious problems remain. The people's lack of trust in their government results from two key factors. First, some GIRoA officials have given preferential treatment to certain individuals, tribes, and groups or worse, abused their power at the expense of the people. Second, the Afghan government has been unable to provide sufficient security, justice, and basic services to the people. Although the capacity and integrity of some Afghan institutions have improved and the number of competent officials has grown, this progress has been insufficient to counter the issues that undermine legitimacy. These problems contribute to the Afghan Government's inability to gain the support of the Afghan population.

ISAF errors also compound the problem. ISAF is not adequately executing the basics of COIN doctrine. Thus the first major recommendation of this assessment is to change and focus on that which ISAF has the most control of: ISAF. The coalition must hold itself accountable before it can attempt to do so with others.

Specifically, ISAF will focus on two major changes to improve execution of COIN fundamentals and enhance organizational alignment and efficacy: ISAF will change its operating culture to pursue a counterinsurgency approach that puts the Afghan people first. While the insurgency can afford to lose fighters and leaders, it cannot afford to lose control of the population.

ISAF must operate differently. Preoccupied with force protection, ISAF has operated in a manner that distances itself, both physically and psychologically, from the people they seek to protect. The Afghan people have paid the price, and the mission has been put at risk. In order to be successful as counterinsurgents, ISAF must alter its operational culture to focus on building personal

Above: Extraction time for a US army patrol following a series of intensive COIN operations.

Right: A convoy of Australian vehicles laager up near an ISAF MSR.

relationships with its Afghan partners and the protected population. To gain accurate information and intelligence about the local environment, ISAF must spend as much time as possible with the people and as little time as possible in armored vehicles or behind the walls of forward operating bases. ISAF personnel must seek out, understand, and act to address the needs and grievances of the people in their local environment. Strong personal relationships forged between security forces and local populations will be a key to success.

ISAF cannot succeed if it is unwilling to share risk, at least equally, with the people. In fact, once the risk is shared, effective force protection will come from the people, and the overall risk can actually be reduced by operating differently. The more coalition forces are seen and known by the local population, the more their threat will be reduced. Adjusting force protection measures to local conditions sends a powerful message of confidence and normalcy to the population. Subordinate commanders must have greater freedom with respect to setting force protection measures they employ in order to help close the gap between security forces and the people they protect. Arguably, giving leaders greater flexibility to adjust force protection measures could expose military personnel and civilians to greater risk in the near term; however, historical experiences in counterinsurgency warfare, coupled with the above, suggests that accepting some risk in the short term will ultimately save lives in the long run.

Reintegration is a normal component of counterinsurgency warfare. It is qualitatively different from reconciliation and is a critical part of the new strategy. As coalition operations proceed, insurgents will have three choices: fight, flee, or reintegrate. ISAF must identify opportunities to reintegrate former mid- to low-level insurgent fighters into normal society by offering them a way out. To do so, ISAF requires a credible program to offer eligible insurgents reasonable incentives to stop fighting and return to normalcy, possibly including the provision of employment and protection.

Such a program will require resources and focus, as appropriate, on people's future rather than past behaviour. ISAF's soldiers will be required to think about COIN operations differently, in that there are now three outcomes instead of two: enemy may be killed, captured, or reintegrated.

A Strategy for Success

Success will be achieved when GIRoA has earned the support of the powerful Afghan people and effectively controls its own territory. This will not come easily or quickly. It is realistic to expect that Afghan and coalition casualties will increase until GIRoA and ISAF regain the initiative. ISAF's strategy to defeat the insurgency and achieve this end state, based on an in depth analysis of the nature of the conflict, includes four major pillars:

ISAF will become radically more integrated and partnered with the ANSF to enable a more rapid expansion of their capacity and responsibility for security.

ISAF will place support to responsive and accountable governance, including subnational and community governance, on par with security.

ISAF's operations will focus first on gaining the initiative and reversing the momentum of the insurgency.

ISAF will prioritize available resources to those critical areas where the population is most threatened.

Afghanistan's Security

The Afghan National Army (ANA) must accelerate growth to the present target strength of 134,000 by Fall 2010 with the institutional flexibility to continue that growth to a new target ceiling of 240,000.The target strength of the Afghan National Police (ANP) must be raised to 160,000. This will require additional mentors, trainers, partners and funds through an expanded participation by GIRoA, the support of ISAF, and the resources of troop nations. The ANP suffers from a lack of training, leaders, resources, equipment, and mentoring. Effective policing is inhibited by the absence of a working system of justice or dispute resolution; poor pay has also encouraged corruption.

Getting the right information and evidence from those detained in military operations is also necessary to support rule of law and reintegration programs and help ensure that only insurgents are detained and civilians are not unduly affected. Detainee operations are both complex and politically sensitive. There are strategic vulnerabilities in a non-Afghan system. By contrast, an Afghan system reinforces their sense of sovereignty and responsibility.

As always, the detention process must be effective in providing key intelligence and avoid 'catch and release' approaches that endanger coalition and ANSF forces. It is therefore imperative to evolve to a more holistic model centred on an Afghan-run system. This will require a comprehensive system that addresses the entire 'life-cycle' and extends from point of capture to eventual reintegration or prosecution.

Learning from and Leveraging the Elections

The recent Presidential and Provincial Council elections were far from perfect. From a security standpoint, they were generally executed smoothly and without major physical disruption, although the credibility of the election results remains an open question. The country-wide spike in violence against

Left: An Australian sniper looks out for possible Taliban activity. In mid-2009 Australian troop deployment was increased by 50% – but that was not as dramatic as it sounds, involving an extra 450, most assigned to train the ANA. The figures do not compare with the US increase from 38,000 to 60,000 personnel.

Below: A group of ISAF vehicles form up for a publicity photo prior to going out on PRT activities.

ISAF and ANSF, with three to four times the average number of attacks, underscores the widespread reach of insurgent influence, particularly in the south and the east and in select areas of the north and west.

However, the relatively low number of effective attacks against polling centres offers some evidence that insurgents were targeting ISAF and ANSF, not the voters. The Afghans' ability to plan and execute the elections, along with the close partnering between ISAF and ANSF, and the mass deployment of security forces were notable achievements nonetheless. The elections were also an opportunity, and a forcing function, that will help to improve future coordination within the ANSF and expand ISAF's partnership with GIRoA and the international community.

Supporting Local Governance

Elements of Afghan society, particularly rural populations, have been excluded from the political process. ISAF must support UNAMA and the international community in sub-national governance reform by working directly with local communities, starting by assessing Afghan civilian needs by population center and developing partnerships to act on them. By empowering local communities, GIRoA, supported by ISAF, can encourage them to support the political system.

Efforts are underway that may address some of these issues, including those that have been cultivated through the National Solidarity Program and the Afghan Social Outreach Program. These structures will enable improvements at the community level to link communities with the national government over time. In addition, GIRoA's proposed sub-national governance policy aims to give greater authority and responsibility to the elected councils and to clarify their relationships with governors and individual line ministries.

Negative Influencers

ISAF must understand and address underlying factors that encourage malign behaviour and undermine governance. The narco- and illicit economy and the extortion associated with large-scale developmental projects undermine the economy in Afghanistan.

Discerning Support

ISAF must develop a discerning approach that rewards competent Afghan governance and leadership, recognizes the distinction between incapacity and predatory behavior, and leverages ISAF's influence to address both challenges. ISAF and its partners must develop appropriate measures to reduce the incentives for corrupt actors that impede the mission, work around them if necessary, and develop actionable evidence of their malfeasance. Improving information collection and analysis will provide better understanding of the motivations, practices, and effects of corruption.

Transparency and Accountability

ISAF must work with UNAMA [United Nations Assistance Mission] and the international community to build public finance mechanisms that enable GIRoA to create credible programs and allocate resources according to the needs of the Afghan people. The international community must address its own corrupt or counter-productive practices, including reducing the amount of development money that goes toward overhead and intermediaries rather than the Afghan people.

A recent OXFAM report indicates that a significant percentage of such funding is diverted. ISAF must pay particular attention to how development projects are contracted and to whom. Too often these projects enrich power-brokers, corrupt officials, or international contractors and serve only limited segments of the population. Improving ISAF's knowledge of the environment and sharing this information with UNAMA and the international community will help mitigate such harmful practices.

ISAF will provide economic support to counterinsurgency operations to help provide a bridge to critical developmental projects in priority areas that UN agencies and the international community cannot reach, while working closely with UNAMA to help set conditions for NGOs to enter stabilized areas.

Rule of Law

Finally, ISAF must work with its civilian and international counterparts to enable justice sector reform and locate resources for formal and informal justice systems that offer swift and fair resolution of disputes, particularly at the local level. The provision of local justice, to include such initiatives as mobile courts, will be a critical enhancement of Afghan capacity in the eyes of the people. ISAF must work with GIRoA to develop a clear mandate and boundaries for local informal justice systems.

First, ISAF must re-focus its operations to gain the initiative in seriously threatened, populated areas by working directly with GIRoA institutions and people in local communities to gain their support and to diminish insurgent access and influence. This stage is clearly decisive to the overall effort. It will require sufficient resources to gain the initiative and definitively check the insurgency. A failure to reverse the momentum of the insurgency will not only preclude success in Afghanistan, it will result in a loss of public and political support outside Afghanistan.

AFGHANISTAN
ISAF RC AND PRT LOCATIONS

Clockwise from top left:

ISAF PRT activities in Afghanistan at the beginning of 2009.

ANA soldier being put through combat training in Kabul.

General David Petraeus, arguably America's finest commander since the Second World War.

A USAF airman repairs a strip of concrete that has worn out from the constant use and abuse that it has been subjected to since 2002.

As ISAF and ANSF capabilities grow over the next 12–24 months and the insurgency diminishes in critical areas, ISAF will begin a second stage – a strategic consolidation. As ANSF and GIRoA increasingly take the lead for security operations and as new civilian and military capacity arrives, security operations will expand to wider areas while consolidating initial gains. These efforts will increase the space in which the population feels protected and served by their government, and insulate them from a return of insurgent influence.

In a country as large and complex as Afghanistan, ISAF cannot be strong everywhere. ISAF must focus its full range of civilian and military resources where they will have the greatest effect on the people. This will generally be in those specific geographical areas that represent key terrain. For the counter-insurgent, the key terrain is generally where the population lives and works. This is also where the insurgents are typically focused; thus, it is here where the population is threatened by the enemy and that the two sides inevitably meet. ISAF will initially focus on critical high-population areas that are contested or controlled by insurgents, not because the enemy is present, but because it is here that the population is threatened by the insurgency.

The geographical deployment of forces may not be static; ISAF must retain the operational flexibility to adapt to changes in the environment. Based on current assessments, ISAF prioritizes the effort in Afghanistan into three categories to guide the allocation of resources. These priorities will evolve over time as conditions on the ground change.

Measuring Progress

ISAF must develop effective assessment architectures, in concert with civilian partners and home nations, to measure the effects of the strategy, assess progress toward key objectives, and make necessary adjustments. ISAF must identify and refine appropriate indicators to assess progress. Because the mission depends on GIRoA, ISAF must also develop clear metrics to assess progress in governance.

Resources and Risk

Proper resourcing will be critical. The campaign in Afghanistan has been historically under-resourced and remains so today – ISAF is operating in a culture of poverty. Consequently, ISAF requires more forces. This increase partially reflects previously validated, yet un-sourced, requirements. This also stems from the new mix of capabilities essential to execute the new strategy.

Some efficiency will be gained through better use of ISAF's existing resources, eliminating redundancy, and the leveraging of ANSF growth, increases in GIRoA capacity, international community resources, and the population itself. Nonetheless, ISAF requires capabilities and resources well in excess of these efficiency gains. The greater resources will not be sufficient to achieve success, but will enable implementation of the new strategy. Conversely, inadequate resources will likely result in failure. However, without a new strategy, the mission should not be resourced. A 'properly-resourced' strategy provides the means deemed necessary to accomplish the mission with appropriate and acceptable risk. In the case of Afghanistan, this level of resourcing is less than the amount that is required to secure the whole country. By comparison, a 'fully-resourced' strategy could achieve low risk, but this would be excessive in the final analysis.

Some areas are more consequential for the survival of GIRoA than others. The determination of what constitutes 'properly-resourced' will be based on force density doctrine applied with best military judgment of factors such as terrain, location and accessibility of the population, intensity of the threats, the effects of ISR capabilities and other enablers, logistical constraints, and historical experience. As always, assessment of risk will necessarily include subjective professional judgment.

Under resourcing COIN is perilous because the insurgent has the advantage of mobility whereas security forces become relatively fixed after securing an area. Force density doctrine is based in historical analysis and suggests that a certain presence of security forces is required to achieve a critical threshold that overmatches the insurgents' ability to leverage their mobility. In short, a 'properly-resourced' strategy places enough things, in enough places, for enough time. All three are mandatory.

A 'properly-resourced' strategy is imperative. Resourcing coalition forces below this level will leave critical areas of Afghanistan open to insurgent influence while the ANSF grows. Thus, the first stage of the strategy will be unachievable, leaving GIRoA and IsAF unable to execute the decisive second stage. In addition, the international community is unlikely to have the access necessary to facilitate effective Afghan governance in contested areas. Failure to provide adequate resources also risks a longer conflict, greater casualties, higher overall costs, and ultimately, a critical loss of political support. Any of these risks, in turn, are likely to result in mission failure.

Civilian Capacity

ISAF cannot succeed without a corresponding cadre of civilian experts to support the change in strategy and capitalize on the expansion and acceleration of counterinsurgency efforts. Effective civilian capabilities and resourcing mechanisms are critical to achieving demonstrable progress. The relative level of civilian resources must be balanced with security forces, lest gains in security outpace civilian capacity for governance and economic improvements. In

Top: An Australian LAV passes the Qalat city outer markers. Qalat in Zabul Province is overlooked by a 19th-century British fortress.

Above: Bagram PRT team handing out stuffed toys to Afghan children.

Right: A soldier from 3rd Battalion Royal Australian Regiment observing the daily Afghan life that passes by in front of him. Insurgent or friend – who knows?

particular, ensuring alignment of resources for immediate and rapid expansion into newly secured areas will require integrated civil-military planning teams that establish mechanisms for rapid response. In addition, extensive work is required to ensure international and host nation partners are engaged and fully integrated.

Incentive to Support the Afghan Government

Some of the additional civilian experts will partner with ISAF task forces or serve on Provincial Reconstruction Teams. Others will work with new District Support Teams as necessary to support this strategy. As necessary, ISAF must facilitate performance of civil-military functions wherever civilian capacity is lacking, the arrival of the civilians is delayed, or the authorities that the civilians bring prove insufficient. ISAF will welcome the introduction of any new civilian funding streams, but must be prepared to make up the difference using military funding as necessary.

Risks

No strategy can guarantee success. A number of risks outside of ISAF's control could undermine the mission, to include a loss of coalition political will, insufficient ability and political will on GIRoA's part to win the support of its people and to control its territory, failure to provide effective civilian capabilities by ISAF's partners, significant improvements or adaptations by insurgent groups, and actions of external actors such as Pakistan and Iran.

Conclusion

The situation in Afghanistan is serious. The mission can be accomplished, but this will require two fundamental changes. First, ISAF must focus on getting the basics right to achieve a new, population-centric operational culture and better unity of effort.

Second, ISAF must also adopt a new strategy, one that is properly resourced, to radically increase partnership with the ANSF, emphasize governance, prioritize resources where the population is threatened, and gain the initiative from the insurgency. This will entail significant near-term cost and risk; however, the long-term risk of not executing this strategy is greater. The U.S. Strategy and NATO mission for Afghanistan both call for a committed and comprehensive approach to the strategic threat of an unsecure and unstable Afghanistan.

Accelerating the growth and development of both the Afghan National Army (ANA) and Afghan National Police (ANP) is a vital part of the strategy to create the conditions for sustainable security and stability in Afghanistan.

Demonstrable progress by the Afghan government and its security forces in countering the insurgency over the next 12 to 18 months is critical in order to preserve the sustained commitment and support of the international community. A key component of success will be the ability of the ANSF to assume progressively greater responsibility for security operations from the deployed international forces. The requirement to expand the ANSF (both ANA and ANP) rapidly to address the challenges of the insurgency will require ISAF to provide enhanced partnering, mentoring, and enabling capabilities until parallel capabilities are developed within the ANSF.

Key Findings

ANA

The ANA has a force structure of nearly 92k and, while still nascent and dependent on enablers provided by international forces, is increasingly capable of leading or conducting independent operations; however, more COIN capable Afghan Army forces are required in order to conduct sustained COIN operations in key areas of the country.

Over the past several years, the ANA has grown in capacity and capability. Late last year a decision to increase the size of the ANA to 134k was followed by a plan from the Afghan Ministry of Defense (supported by CSTC-A) [Combined Security Transition Command] to accelerate the training of 8 Kandaks in order to enhance security in key areas, mainly in Southern Afghanistan. That acceleration is currently ongoing.

The growth of the ANA to 134k needs to be brought forward from December 2011 to October 2010 in order to create sufficient ANA capacity to create conditions for rapid and sustainable progress in the current campaign; however, there is a requirement for further substantial growth (to an estimated end strength of 240k) of COIN capable ANA troops in order to increase pressure on the insurgency in threatened areas in the country. In order to generate the required numbers of 'boots on the ground,' the emphasis will be on the development of manoeuvre units rather than enabler capabilities.

The generation of previously planned and programmed enablers such as corps engineers, artillery, motorized quick reaction forces, and large support battalions will be deferred to enable a more rapid generation of manoeuvre forces that provide the operational capabilities required now. The forces generated during this phase will have sufficient training, capability and equipment to conduct effective COIN operations and to generate momentum. Tighter, restructured training programs will deliver an infantry-based, COIN capable, force in a shorter period of time with the capability of conducting 'hold' operations with some 'clear' capability while closely partnered with coalition

Canadian artillery in action.

forces. These forces will be equipped at a 'minimally combat essential' level as determined by the Ministry of Defense, ISAF's operational requirements, and CSTC-A's ability to generate forces. More inexperienced leaders will be accepted into the junior officer and NCO ranks and the risk will be balanced by close partnering ANSF with coalition forces.

Finally, the Afghan National Army Air Corps will continue to grow and develop at a measured pace, given the long lead times required for the acquisition of aircraft and development of technical skills to operate and maintain the aircraft in the inventory. In the short term, the accelerated acquisition of additional Mi-17 airframes will enable greater lift capacity for the ANSF. In parallel, dedicated training of Mi-35 aircrews will add a rotary wing attack capability in the fall of 2009. Deliveries of the first C-27 aircraft in November 2009 will dramatically increase operational capability as the first crews are trained in March 2010.

ANP

The Afghan National Police has grown to a current force structure of approximately 84k and is several years behind the ANA in its development. Due to a lack of overall strategic coherence and insufficient resources, the ANP has not been organized, trained, and equipped to operate effectively as a counter-insurgency force. Promising programs to reform and train police have proceeded too slowly due to a lack of training teams. To enhance the ANP's capacity and capabilities, the Focused District Development (FDD) program must be accelerated to organize, train, equip, and reform police that have not yet completed a formal program of instruction, and new police forces such as the elite Afghan National Civil Order Police (ANCOP) must be generated to prepare the ANP properly to operate in this challenging COIN environment.

The ANP must increase in size in order to provide sufficient police needed to hold areas that have been cleared of insurgents, and to increase the capacity to secure the population. This assessment recommends further growth of the ANP to a total of 160k as soon as practicable with the right mix of capabilities that better satisfies the requirements of a counter-insurgency effort. This larger number of policemen also needs to be trained more quickly in order to 'thicken' security forces in the districts, provinces, and regions.

Subsequent ANP growth to 160k will include doubling ANP strength at the District and Provincial levels, significantly increasing the police-to-population ratio. The growth of ANCOP will be accelerated by generating 5 national battalions in FY'10 followed by the generation of 34 new provincial battalions and 6 new regional battalions. While the number of ABP [Afghan Border Police] companies will remain the same, each ABP company will increase in strength by 65% to 150 men per company.

Finally, the Afghan Public Protection Force (APPF) personnel will be absorbed into the ANP as it expands. Over the 4 year program, special police growth will provide important niche capabilities. The national Crisis Response Unit (CRU) will provide Assault, Surveillance, and Support squadrons. Counter-Narcotics Aviation is projected to grow by over 100%. Afghan Special Narcotics forces grow by 25%. Security forces will also be provided to ensure international and non-governmental organizations' freedom of movement.

Recommendations

1. Grow the ANA to a target authorization of 240k. Accelerate the growth of the currently approved COIN focused infantry force of 134K by late 2010 and generate more counter-insurgency forces consistent with operational requirements.

2. Grow and develop the ANP to a total of 160k as soon as practicable to 'thicken and harden' security in the districts, provinces, regions. This total will also more than double the size of Afghan Border Police, considerably grow ANCOP and allow for expansion of the Afghan Public Protection Force where appropriate.

3. Realign and streamline the responsibilities for ANSF generation and development: CSTC-A/NATO Training Mission-Afghanistan (NTM-A) focuses on ANSF force generation consistent with operational requirements, develops Afghan ministerial and institutional capabilities, and resources the fielded forces. Shift responsibility for development of fielded ANSF to the JC. Employ enhanced partnering and mentoring to more rapidly develop Afghan forces.

4. Provide CSTC-A direct authority to obligate Afghan Security Forces Funding (ASFF) without passing actions through the Defense Security Cooperation Agency to shorten capabilities procurement timelines and avoid unnecessary fees.

5. Shift the responsibility and authority for execution of all police training from the Department of State's Bureau of International Narcotics and Law Enforcement (INL) to CSTC-A to enhance unity of effort in police development.

CSTC-A will assume operational control of INL contracted trainers as soon as possible until January 2010 when a new contract managed by CSTC-A can begin.

Top from left to right:

A British logistics convoy making its way through a poppy field. Of particular interest is that at the time the photograph was taken, it still had not been harvested – which probably indicated that there was an over-supply of the crop.

Colonel Rasoul of the Afghan Army.

Royal Marines from 42 CDO on patrol during Operation Diesel.

Right: CV 90s bombing up for a mission.

Below: A Danish Leopard on Operation Son Chara.

X

FINAL THOUGHTS

As I write these final pages the streets of Pakistan are running with blood – not from any major battle, but the result of murder, courtesy of the Taliban and Al-Qaeda – their response to Pakistan's military offensive against them in Waziristan. I actually believe the perpetrators of this mass murder do not know any more what it is they are fighting for. Why? Because the victims of these bloody attacks were mostly Pakistanis – fellow Muslims that follow the teaching of the Koran, just like them.

They say that when politicians start turning on their own kind it is a sign that they know their number is up. But does that apply to the Taliban? Well on the face of it, Taliban inc seems busier than ever – both in Pakistan and Afghanistan – and its membership has grown substantially in recent years. Yet I cannot help thinking that despite the strong front they show us, behind the scenes all is not well. There are signs that the Taliban is hurting on all sides and that in due course as a consequence it will loosen its grip on Afghanistan; but not just yet. If we look at the Taliban from a purely military point of view it cannot prevail in conventional symmetric warfare against the forces of ISAF, as we saw in 2002 – which leaves only asymmetric warfare. And to win in this form of warfare it must be able to either hide amongst the population, or if that is not possible then it must fight from neighbouring countries. These options of course assume that those who give them shelter and succour are sympathetic towards their cause. But what if they are not? Then the only option open to the Taliban is forcing themselves upon the population by means of coercion and intimidation. What if this last option is denied to them by NATO? Then there could only be one possible outcome for them. Defeat.

This makes it sound all so easy – which of course it is not. Just trying to get the Coalition Allies to embark on a consistent, committed strategy in Afghanistan is a battle in itself. But these principles, if applied, would work, it is a question of implementing them. In my opinion, if we win the battle for the hearts and minds of the Afghan people then we win the battle for Afghanistan.

As for Al-Qaeda, most of them left Afghanistan long ago, setting up shop instead in Waziristan, Yemen and Somalia. The West does not appear to have fully appreciated that fact. Perhaps the war against them has not really begun yet, as we have been sidetracked in Afghanistan fighting a war against the Taliban that maybe we should not have started.

A Royal Marine Lynx departs for another mission over Helmand. Although fast and agile over England's pleasant green pastures, it struggles in the hot and high conditions of Afghanistan.

Above: 30 A US Blackhawk departs a remote FOB (Forward Operations Base). Helicopters are of course vital to their survival, as troops and supplies can be brought in far more safely and efficiently than would be the case with a road vehicle.

Below: A US Army Chinook deploys its load near a snowy Bagram.

Below left: Dutch Army Sgt Major with tribal representative.

Left: Dutch patrol near Mirabad.

XI

THE FALLEN

This chapter is dedicated to the memory of all the brave men and women of our armed forces and those of our NATO allies who have given their today for Afghanistan's tomorrow. Their sacrifice will never be forgotten.

As at 7 December 2009, a total of 237 British forces personnel or MOD civilians have died while serving in Afghanistan since the start of operations in October 2001.Of these, 206 were killed as a result of hostile action. 31 are known to have died either as a result of illness, non-combat injuries or accidents, or have not yet officially been assigned a cause of death pending the outcome of an investigation. The balance of these figures may change as inquests are concluded.

Lance Corporal **Adam Paul Drane** aged 23 from Bury St Edmunds of 1st Battalion The Royal Anglian Regiment was killed in Afghanistan on Monday 7 December 2009.

Acting Sergeant **John Paxton Amer** from Sunderland of 1st Battalion Coldstream Guards died from wounds sustained as a result of an explosion that happened in the Babaji area of central Helmand province on 30 November 2009.

Sergeant **Robert David Loughran-Dickson** aged 33 from Deal in Kent of the Royal Military Police died as a result of gunshot wounds sustained during a routine patrol in the vicinity of Patrol Base Wahid, in Nad e-Ali district, Helmand province, on 18 November 2009.

Corporal **Loren Owen Christopher Marlton-Thomas** aged 28 of 33 Engineer Regiment (EOD) was killed by an improvised explosive device in the Gereshk area of Helmand province on Sunday 15 November 2009.

Rifleman **Andrew Ian Fentiman** aged 23 from Cambridge of 7th Battalion The Rifles was killed as a result of small arms fire whilst on a foot patrol near Sangin in central Helmand province during the morning of 15 November 2009.

Rifleman **Samuel John Bassett** aged 20 from Plymouth of 4th Battalion The Rifles was killed following an improvised explosive device explosion in the area of Sangin on Sunday 8 November 2009.

Rifleman **Philip Allen** aged 20 from Dorset of 2nd Battalion The Rifles (2 RIFLES), was killed following the detonation of an IED near Sangin in central Helmand province on Saturday 7 November 2009.

Serjeant **Phillip Scott** aged 30 from Malton of 3rd Battalion The Rifles was killed in Afghanistan following an improvised explosive device explosion in northern Helmand province on Thursday 5 November 2009.

Warrant Officer Class 1 (RSM) **Darren Chant** aged 40 from Walthamstow, Sergeant **Matthew Telford** aged 37 from Grimsby and Guardsman **James Major** aged 18 from Grimsby, all of the 1st Battalion The Grenadier Guards as well as Acting Corporal **Steven Boote** aged 22 from Birkenhead, Liverpool and Corporal **Nicholas Webster-Smith** aged 24 from Glangwilli, both of the Royal Military Police were killed as a result of gunshot wounds sustained in an attack at a police checkpoint in the Nad e-Ali district of Helmand province on Tuesday 3 November 2009.

Staff Sergeant **Olaf Sean George Schmid** aged 30 from Truro of the Royal Logistic Corps, in Afghanistan on the afternoon of Saturday 31 October 2009.

Corporal **Thomas 'Tam' Mason** aged 27 from Rosyth of The Black Watch, 3rd Battalion The Royal Regiment of Scotland (3 SCOTS), at the Royal Centre for Defence Medicine, Selly Oak Hospital, on Sunday 25 October 2009.

Corporal **James Oakland** aged 26 from Manchester of the Royal Military Police was killed as a result of an explosion that happened during a foot patrol near to Gereshk district centre in central Helmand province on Thursday 22 October 2009.

Lance Corporal **James Hill** aged 23 from Redhill in Surrey of 1st Battalion Coldstream Guards was killed as a result of an explosion near Camp Bastion in Helmand Province on Thursday 8 October 2009.

Guardsman **Jamie Janes** aged 20 from Brighton of the 1st Battalion Grenadier Guards, was killed as a result of an explosion that happened whilst on a foot patrol near to Nad e-Ali district centre in central Helmand province on Monday 5 October 2009.

Acting Corporal **Marcin Wojtak** aged 24 from Leicester of 34 Squadron Royal Air Force Regiment was killed as a result of an explosion whilst commanding his vehicle in the desert to the south of Bastion Joint Operating Base on Thursday 1 October 2009.

Private **James Prosser** aged 21 from Cwmbran of 2nd Battalion The Royal Welsh was killed as a result of an explosion that happened during a vehicle patrol in Musa Qaleh district, northern Helmand province on 27 September 2009.

Acting Sergeant **Michael Lockett** MC from Monifieth in Angus of 2nd Battalion The Mercian Regiment was killed in Afghanistan as a result of an explosion

French soldiers on patrol. At the end of 2009 France had around 3,000 troops stationed mainly north of Kabul in the Kapisa and Surobi areas. In November that year insurgents targetted Brig. Gen. Marcel Druart, Commander of the the French task force, as he met with tribal elders from the Tagreb Valley in a crowded market place. Two Chinese-made Chicom rockets killed three children and wounded 20 other people. The General was not hit.

while on a foot patrol in the Gereshk district of Helmand province on 21 September 2009.

Acting Serjeant **Stuart McGrath** aged 28 from Buckinghamshire of 2nd Battalion The Rifles was killed as a result of an explosion that happened whilst on a foot patrol in the Gereshk district, central Helmand province, on the afternoon of 16 September 2009.

Trooper **Brett Hall** aged 21 from Dartmouth of the 2nd Royal Tank Regiment died at the Royal Centre for Defence Medicine, Selly Oak, on Wednesday 16 September 2009 of wounds sustained in Afghanistan.

Kingsman **Jason Dunn-Bridgeman** aged 20 from Liverpool of 2nd Battalion The Duke of Lancaster's Regiment was killed in a firefight with the enemy during a foot patrol in the Babaji district of Helmand province on 13 September 2009.

Corporal **John Harrison** from The Parachute Regiment was killed in Afghanistan on Wednesday 9 September 2009.

Private **Gavin Elliott** aged 19 from Woodsetts, Worksop, Nottinghamshire of 2nd Battalion The Mercian Regiment died as a result of a gunshot wound sustained whilst on a foot patrol in Babaji district, central Helmand province, on Thursday 3 September 2009.

Lance Corporal **Richard James Brandon** aged 24 from Kidderminster of the Corps of Royal Electrical and Mechanical Engineers was killed in Afghanistan on 2 September 2009.

Sergeant **Stuart Millar** aged 40 from Inverness and Private **Kevin Elliott** aged 24 from Dundee of The Black Watch, 3rd Battalion The Royal Regiment of Scotland, were killed as a result of an explosion believed to have been caused by a rocket-propelled grenade whilst patrolling on foot in Babaji district, Helmand province, on the morning of Monday 31 August 2009.

Sergeant **Lee Andrew Houltram**, Royal Marines, died following an explosion whilst on a foot patrol near Gereshk in Helmand province, Afghanistan, in the early hours of Saturday 29 August 2009.

Fusilier **Shaun Bush** aged 24 from Warwickshire of 2nd Battalion The Royal Regiment of Fusiliers died at the Royal Centre for Defence Medicine, Selly Oak, on Tuesday 25 August 2009, having been wounded in an explosion while on a foot patrol in Sangin district, Helmand province, on Saturday 15 August 2009.

Serjeant **Paul McAleese** aged 29 from Hereford of 2nd Battalion the Rifles, and Private **Johnathon Young** aged 18 from Hull of 3rd Battalion The Yorkshire Regiment (Duke of Wellington's), were killed in Afghanistan on Thursday 20 August 2009 following explosions that happened while they were on a foot patrol taking place in Sangin district.

Lance Corporal **James Fullarton** aged 24 from Coventry, Fusilier Simon Annis from Salford and Fusilier Louis Carter from Nuneaton, all of 2nd Battalion The Royal Regiment of Fusiliers, were killed in Afghanistan on Sunday 16 August 2009.

Sergeant **Simon Valentine** aged 29 from Bedworth of 2nd Battalion The Royal Regiment of Fusiliers was killed in Afghanistan on Saturday 15 August 2009.

Private **Richard Hunt** aged 21 from Abergavenny of 2nd Battalion The Royal Welsh died at the Royal Centre for Defence Medicine in Selly Oak on Saturday 15 August 2009 from wounds sustained in Helmand province two days previously.

Captain **Mark Hale** aged 42 from Bournemouth and Rifleman **Daniel Wild** aged 19 from Hartlepool of 2nd Battalion The Rifles and Lance Bombardier **Matthew Hatton** aged 23 from Easingwold in North Yorkshire of 40th Regiment Royal Artillery (The Lowland Gunners) were killed in Afghanistan on Thursday 13 August 2009.

Private **Jason George Williams** aged 23 from Worcester of 2nd Battalion The Mercian Regiment was killed in Afghanistan on Saturday 8 August 2009.

Corporal **Kevin Mulligan** aged 26, Lance Corporal **Dale Thomas Hopkins** aged 23 and Private **Kyle Adams** aged 21 from The Parachute Regiment were killed when the vehicle they were travelling in was hit by an explosion to the north of Lashkar Gah on 6 August 2009.

Craftsman **Anthony Lombardi** aged 21 from Scunthorpe of the Royal Electrical and Mechanical Engineers (REME), attached to The Light Dragoons, was killed when his vehicle was hit by an explosion in the Lashkar Gah district of Helmand province on 4 August 2009.

Trooper **Phillip Lawrence** aged 22 from Birkenhead of The Light Dragoons died in an explosion in Lashkar Gah district, on 27 July 2009.

Warrant Officer Class 2 **Sean Upton** aged 35 from Nottinghamshire of 5th Regiment Royal Artillery was killed as a result of an explosion in Sangin district, Helmand province on 27 July 2009.

Bombardier **Craig Hopson** aged 24 from Castleford of 40th Regiment Royal Artillery (The Lowland Gunners) was killed following an improvised explosive device explosion on 25 July 2009.

Guardsman **Christopher King** aged 20 from Birkenhead, near Liverpool of 1st Battalion Coldstream Guards, was killed following an improvised explosive device explosion in the Nad e-Ali district, Helmand province, on 22 July 2009.

Captain **Daniel Shepherd** aged 28 from Lincoln of 11 Explosive Ordnance Disposal Regiment, The Royal Logistic Corps, was killed following an explosion in Nad e-Ali district, Helmand province, on Monday 20 July 2009.

Corporal **Joseph Etchells** aged 22 from Mossley of 2nd Battalion The Royal Regiment of Fusiliers was killed as a result of an explosion during a foot patrol near Sangin, northern Helmand province, on Sunday 19 July 2009.

Rifleman **Aminiasi Toge** aged 26 from Suva, Fiji of 2nd Battalion The Rifles was killed as a result of an explosion that happened whilst he was conducting a foot patrol close to Forward Operating Base Keenan, near Gereshk in central Helmand province on Thursday 16 July 2009.

Above: Tribal elders await the arrival of an ISAF patrol.

Below: Everyday life in an Afghan village – something ISAF are fighting to defend.

Clockwise from top:

Norwegian convoy out on patrol.

Afghan children looking happy enough outside a local school. Such a scene in the West would be taken for granted. In Afghanistan it is highly prized – as blood has flowed to make it possible.

Soldiers from the Black Watch hold a shura with village elders.

Gurkhas with Afghan National Police conduct a combined patrol.

Corporal **Jonathan Horne** aged 28 from Walsall, Rifleman **William Aldridge** aged 18 from Bromyard in Herefordshire, Rifleman **James Backhouse** aged 18 from Castleford, Yorkshire, Rifleman **Joseph Murphy** aged 18 from Castle Bromwich, Birmingham and Rifleman **Daniel Simpson** aged 20 from Croydon, all of 2nd Battalion The Rifles, were killed in action near Forward Operating Base Wishtan, Sangin on Friday 10 July 2009.

Corporal **Lee Scott** aged 26 from Kings Lynn of The 2nd Royal Tank Regiment was killed during an explosion just north of Nad Ali, Helmand Province, on the morning of Friday 10 July 2009.

Private **John Brackpool** aged 27 from Crawley, West Sussex, serving as a rifleman with the Prince of Wales' Company, 1st Battalion Welsh Guards, was killed whilst on operations near Char-e-Anjir, just outside Lashkar Gah, in Helmand Province on 9 July 2009.

Rifleman **Daniel Hume** of 4th Battalion The Rifles was killed in a contact explosion whilst on a foot patrol near Nad e-Ali, Helmand province on 9 July 2009.

Trooper **Christopher Whiteside** aged 20 from Blackpool of The Light Dragoons was killed in Afghanistan on 7 July 2009.

Captain **Ben Babington-Browne** aged 27 from Maidstone of 22 Engineer Regiment, Royal Engineers, died in a helicopter crash in Afghanistan on Monday 6 July 2009.

Lance Corporal **Dane Elson** aged 22 from Bridgend of the 1st Battalion Welsh Guards was killed in Afghanistan on 5 July 2009.

Lance Corporal **David Dennis** aged 29 from Llanelli, Wales of The Light Dragoons and Private **Robert Laws** aged 18 from Bromsgrove in Worcestershire of 2nd Battalion The Mercian Regiment were killed in Afghanistan on 4 July 2009.

Lieutenant Colonel **Rupert Thorneloe** MBE, Commanding Officer of the 1st Battalion Welsh Guards, and Trooper **Joshua Hammond** of the 2nd Royal Tank Regiment were killed by an explosion whilst on convoy along the Shamalan Canal, near Lashkar Gah, in Helmand province, Afghanistan, on Wednesday 1 July 2009.

Major **Sean Birchall** aged 33 of the 1st Battalion Welsh Guards, was killed by an explosion whilst on patrol in Basharan, near Lashkar Gah, in Helmand province, Afghanistan on 19 June 2009.

Lieutenant **Paul Mervis** aged 27 from London of 2nd Battalion The Rifles was killed as a result of an explosion during a deliberate operation near Sangin, northern Helmand province, Afghanistan, on the morning of 12 June 2009.

Private **Robert McLaren** aged 20, from the Isle of Mull of The Black Watch, 3rd Battalion The Royal Regiment of Scotland, was killed in Afghanistan on Wednesday 11 June 2009.

Rifleman **Cyrus Thatcher** aged 19, from Reading of 2nd Battalion The Rifles was killed as a result of an explosion whilst he was on a patrol near Gereshk on Tuesday 2 June 2009.

Lance Corporal **Nigel Moffett** aged 28 from Belfast of The Light Dragoons and Corporal **Stephen Bolger** of The Parachute Regiment were killed as a result of an explosion near Musa Qaleh on Saturday 30 May 2009.

Lance Corporal **Kieron Hill** aged 20 from Nottingham of 2nd Battalion The Mercian Regiment (Worcesters and Foresters) was killed following an explosion in Afghanistan on Thursday 28 May 2009.

Lance Corporal **Robert Martin Richards** aged 24 from Betws-y-Coed, North Wales of Armoured Support Group Royal Marines died in Selly Oak Hospital on Wednesday 27 May 2009, from wounds sustained in Helmand five days before.

Sapper **Jordan Rossi** aged 22 from West Yorkshire of 25 Field Squadron, 38 Engineer Regiment, was killed following an explosion in Afghanistan on Saturday 23 May 2009.

Fusilier **Petero 'Pat' Suesue** aged 28 from Fiji of the 2nd Battalion The Royal Regiment of Fusiliers, was killed by an enemy gunshot in Afghanistan on Friday 22 May 2009.

Marine **Jason Mackie** aged 21 from Bampton, Oxfordshire of Armoured Support Group Royal Marines was killed when his vehicle struck an explosive device in the Basharan area of central Helmand on Thursday 14 May 2009.

Lieutenant **Mark Lawrence Evison** aged 26 of 1st Battalion Welsh Guards died of wounds sustained in Afghanistan at Selly Oak Hospital in Birmingham on 12 May 2009.

Sergeant **Ben Ross** of 173 Provost Company, 3rd Regiment, Royal Military Police and Corporal **Kumar Pun** of The 1st Battalion The Royal Gurkha Rifles were killed as a result of a suicide improvised explosive device during a patrol in Gereshk, Helmand province on 7 May 2009.

Rifleman **Adrian Sheldon** from Kirkby-in-Ashfield of 2nd Battalion The Rifles was killed as a result of an explosion near Sangin in Helmand province on Thursday 7 May 2009.

Corporal **Sean Binnie** aged 22 of The Black Watch, 3rd Battalion The Royal Regiment of Scotland (3 SCOTS), was killed near Musa Qaleh in Helmand province on Thursday 7 May 2009.

Lance Sergeant **Tobie Fasfous** aged 29 of 1st Battalion Welsh Guards was killed in Afghanistan on 28 April 2009.

Corporal **Dean Thomas John** aged 25 from Neath and Corporal **Graeme Stiff** aged 24 from Münster, Germany, both of the Royal Electrical and Mechanical Engineers (REME), were killed in southern Afghanistan on Sunday 15 March 2009.

Lance Corporal **Christopher Harkett** aged 22 from Swansea of 2nd Battalion The Royal Welsh was killed in Afghanistan on 14 March 2009.

Clockwise from above:

British troops getting a re-supply courtesy of the RAF.

British troops burn poppy resin following a raid during Op Diesel.

British Sappers at work along the Shamalan canal.

The results of an intensive ISAF search.

US Marine cautiously
making his way
through a potential
ambush area.

Marine **Michael 'Mick' Laski** aged 21 from Liverpool of 45 Commando Royal Marines died of wounds sustained in Afghanistan at Selly Oak Hospital in Birmingham on 25 February 2009.

Corporal **Tom Gaden** aged 24 from Taunton, Lance Corporal **Paul Upton** aged 31 from Paderborn and Rifleman **Jamie Gunn** aged 21 from Leamington Spa, all of 1st Battalion The Rifles, were killed in southern Afghanistan on 25 February 2009.

Lance Corporal **Stephen Kingscott** aged 22 from Plymouth of 1st Battalion The Rifles was killed in Helmand province on 16 February 2009.

Marine **Darren Smith** aged 27 from Fleetwood, Lancashire of 45 Commando Royal Marines was killed on operations in Helmand province on 14 February 2009.

Corporal **Daniel 'Danny' Nield** aged 31 from Cheltenham of 1st Battalion The Rifles, was killed in Helmand province on 30 January 2009.

Acting Corporal **Richard 'Robbo' Robinson** aged 21 from Cornwall of 1st Battalion The Rifles, was killed in Helmand province on 17 January 2009.

Captain **Tom Sawyer** aged 26 from Hertfordshire of 29 Commando Regiment Royal Artillery, and Corporal **Danny Winter** aged 28 from Stockport of 45 Commando Royal Marines, were killed in Afghanistan on 14 January 2009.

Marine **Travis Mackin** aged 22 from Plymouth of Communications Squadron, United Kingdom Landing Force Command Support Group (UKLFCSG), operating as part of 45 Commando Royal Marines, was killed in the Kajaki area of Helmand province on 11 January 2009.

Serjeant **Chris Reed** aged 25 from Plymouth of 6th Battalion The Rifles was killed in action in the Garmsir District of Helmand province on 1 January 2009.

Corporal **Liam Elms** aged 26 from Wigan of 45 Commando Royal Marines, was killed in the Sangin district, Helmand province on 31 December 2008.

Lance Corporal **Benjamin Whatley** aged 20 from King's Lynn of 42 Commando Royal Marines, was killed in Afghanistan on 24 December 2008.

Corporal **Robert Deering** aged 33 from Solihull, Commando Logistic Regiment Royal Marines, was killed in Afghanistan on Sunday 21 December 2008.

Rifleman **Stuart Nash** aged 21 from Sydney, Australia of 1st Battalion The Rifles was killed in Afghanistan on Wednesday 17 December 2008.

Lieutenant **Aaron Lewis** aged 26 from Essex of 29 Commando Regiment Royal Artillery was killed in Afghanistan on 15 December 2008.

Lance Corporal **Steven 'Jamie' Fellows** aged 28 from Sheffield of 45 Commando Royal Marines was killed in the Sangin area of Helmand province on 12 December 2008.

Marine **Damian Davies** aged 27 from Telford, Shropshire, Sergeant **John Manuel** aged 38 from Gateshead, Tyne & Wear and Corporal **Marc Birch** aged 26 from Northampton were killed in the Sangin area of Helmand province on 12 December 2008.

Marine **Tony Evans** aged 20 from Sunderland and Marine **Georgie Sparks** aged 19 from Epping, both of 42 Commando Royal Marines, were killed north-west of Lashkar Gar in southern Helmand province on 27 November 2008.

Marine **Alexander Lucas** aged 24 from Edinburgh of 45 Commando Royal Marines was killed in the Kajaki area of Helmand province on Monday 24 November 2008.

Colour Sergeant **Krishnabahadur Dura** aged 36, from the Lamjung district of western Nepal of the 2nd Battalion The Royal Gurkha Rifles, was killed in Afghanistan on Saturday 15 November 2008.

Marine **Neil David Dunstan** aged 32 from Bournemouth and Marine **Robert Joseph McKibben** aged 32 from County Mayo were killed in Garmsir district, southern Helmand province, on Wednesday 12 November 2008.

Rifleman **Yubraj Rai** aged 28 from Khotang district in eastern Nepal of the 2nd Battalion, The Royal Gurkha Rifles was killed in Afghanistan on Tuesday 4 November 2008.

Trooper **James Munday** aged 21 of D Squadron, the Household Cavalry Regiment (HCR), was killed in southern Afghanistan on 15 October 2008.

Lance Corporal **Nicky Mason** aged 26 from Aveley in Essex of 2nd Battalion The Parachute Regiment, was killed in southern Afghanistan on Saturday 13 September 2008.

Private **Jason Lee Rawstron** aged 23 from Lancashire of 2nd Battalion The Parachute Regiment was killed when his patrol were engaged in an exchange of fire near Forward Operating Base GIBRALTAR on 12 September 2008.

Warrant Officer Class 2 **Gary 'Gaz' O'Donnell** GM aged 40 from Edinburgh of 11 Explosive Ordnance Disposal Regiment Royal Logistic Corps was killed in an explosion in Musa Qaleh, Helmand province on Wednesday 10 September 2008.

Ranger **Justin James Cupples** aged 29 from County Cavan, Ireland of 1st Battalion The Royal Irish Regiment was killed in Sangin town, northern Helmand on Thursday 4 September 2008.

Corporal **Barry Dempsey** aged 29 from Ayrshire of The Royal Highland Fusiliers, 2nd Battalion Royal Regiment of Scotland was killed in the Gereshk area of Helmand province on Monday 18 August 2008.

Signaller **Wayne Bland** aged 21 from Leeds of 16 Signal Regiment was killed in Kabul, Afghanistan on 11 August 2008.

Private **Peter Joe Cowton** aged 25 from Basingstoke of 2nd Battalion The Parachute Regiment was killed in Afghanistan on 29 July 2008.

Sergeant **Jonathan William Mathews** aged 35 from Edinburgh of The Highlanders, 4th Battalion, The Royal Regiment of Scotland was killed in Afghanistan on 28 July 2008.

Above: Dutch armour attached to Task Force Uruzgan.

Below: Dutch troops on patrol with Task Force Uruzgan.

US Marines on foot patrol in Helmand.

Lance Corporal **Kenneth Michael Rowe** aged 24 from Newcastle of the Royal Army Veterinary Corps, attached to 2nd Battalion, The Parachute Regiment, was killed in Afghanistan on Thursday 24 July 2008.

Corporal **Jason Stuart Barnes** aged 25 from Exeter of the Royal Electrical and Mechanical Engineers was killed in southern Afghanistan on Tuesday 22 July 2008.

Lance Corporal **James Johnson** aged 31 from Scotland of B Company, 5th Battalion The Royal Regiment of Scotland was killed while part of a vehicle checkpoint patrol operating in the Lashkar Gar area on Saturday 28 June 2008.

Warrant Officer 2nd Class **Dan Shirley** aged 32 from Leicester of 13 Air Assault Support Regiment, Royal Logistics Corps was killed while on a Logistic Patrol from Sangin to Camp Bastion when the vehicle he was travelling in rolled over on Friday 27 June 2008.

Warrant Officer 2nd Class **Michael Williams** aged 40 from Cardiff of 2nd Battalion The Parachute Regiment (2 PARA) and Private **Joe Whittaker** aged 20 from Stratford Upon Avon of 4th Battalion The Parachute Regiment were killed in Helmand Province, Afghanistan on Tuesday 24 June 2008.

Corporal **Sarah Bryant** aged 26 from Liverpool, Corporal **Sean Reeve** aged 28, Lance Corporal **Richard Larkin** aged 39 and **Paul Stout** aged 31 were killed near Lashkar Gah in Helmand province on Tuesday 17 June 2008.

Lance Corporal **James Bateman** aged 29 from Staines, Middlesex and Private **Jeff Doherty** aged 20 from Southam, Warwickshire, both of 2nd Battalion The Parachute Regiment, were killed in Helmand Province, Afghanistan on Thursday 12 June 2008.

Private **Nathan Cuthbertson** aged 19 from Sunderland, Private **Daniel Gamble** aged 22 from Uckfield, East Sussex and Private Charles Murray aged 19 from Carlisle of 2nd Battalion The Parachute Regiment (2 PARA) were killed when their patrol suffered a suicide explosive device on Sunday 8 June 2008 in Helmand Province, Afghanistan.

Marine **Dale Gostick** aged 22 from Oxford of 3 Troop Armoured Support Company, Royal Marines was killed near Sangin, Helmand province on 25 May 2008.

James Thompson aged 27 from Whitley Bay in Northumberland was killed in the Musa Qaleh area of Afghanistan on 19 May 2008.

Trooper **Ratu Sakeasi Babakobau** aged 29 from Fiji of the Household Cavalry Regiment was killed in Helmand, Afghanistan, on 2 May 2008.

Trooper **Robert Pearson** aged 22 from Grimsby of the Queen's Royal Lancers Regiment was killed in Afghanistan on 21 April 2008.

Senior Aircraftman **Graham Livingstone** aged 23 from Glasgow of the Royal Air Force Regiment and Senior Aircraftman **Gary Thompson** aged 51 from Nottingham of the Royal Auxiliary Air Force Regiment died when the vehicle they were travelling in was caught in an explosion in Kandahar Province on Sunday 13 April 2008.

Lieutenant **John Thornton** aged 22 from Ferndown and Marine **David Marsh** aged 23 from Sheffield, both of 40 Commando Royal Marines, died when the vehicle they were travelling in was caught in an explosion in the vicinity of Kajaki, Helmand province on Sunday 30 March 2008.

Corporal **Damian Mulvihill** aged 32 from Plymouth of 40 Commando Royal Marines was killed in an explosion while taking part in an outreach patrol to disrupt enemy forces north of Sangin in Helmand province on Wednesday 20 February 2008.

Corporal **Damian Stephen Lawrence** aged 25 from Whitby of 2nd Battalion The Yorkshire Regiment (Green Howards) was killed during a joint UK–Afghan National Army night patrol in Kajaki in Helmand province, southern Afghanistan on Sunday 17 February 2008.

Corporal **Darryl Gardiner** (REME) aged 25 from Salisbury in Wiltshire of Royal Electrical and Mechanical Engineers was killed near the town of Musa Qaleh in Helmand province, southern Afghanistan on Sunday 20 January 2008.

Sergeant **Lee Johnson** aged 33 from Stockton-on-Tees of 2nd Battalion The Yorkshire Regiment (Green Howards) was killed in southern Afghanistan on Saturday 8 December 2007.

Trooper **Jack Sadler** aged 21 from Exeter of The Honourable Artillery Company was killed in an explosion in southern Afghanistan on 4 December 2007.

Captain **John McDermid** aged 43 from Glasgow of The Royal Highland Fusiliers, 2nd Battalion The Royal Regiment of Scotland, was killed in southern Afghanistan on Wednesday 14 November 2007.

Lance Corporal **Jake Alderton** aged 22 from Bexley of 36 Engineer Regiment died in southern Afghanistan on Friday 9 November 2007 the vehicle he was travelling in left the road and rolled off a bridge.

Major **Alexis Roberts** aged 32 from Kent serving with 1st Battalion The Royal Gurkha Rifles (but usually an Officer of 2nd Battalion RGR) died as a result of an improvised explosive device in southern Afghanistan on Thursday 4 October 2007.

Colour Sergeant **Phillip Newman** aged 36 from Wolston, Warwickshire of 4th Battalion The Mercian Regiment, and Private **Brian Tunnicliffe** aged 33 from Ilkeston of 2nd Battalion The Mercian Regiment (Worcesters and Foresters), died in a tragic accident in southern Afghanistan on Thursday 20 September 2007.

Corporal **Ivano Violino** aged 29 from Salford from 36 Engineer Regiment died in Helmand province, southern Afghanistan on Monday 17 September 2007.

Sergeant **Craig Brelsford** aged 25 from Nottingham and Private **Johan Botha** from South Africa, both from 2nd Battalion The Mercian Regiment (Worcesters and Foresters), were killed in Helmand Province on Saturday 8 September 2007.

Graphic depicting the enormous amount of logistics support required to keep British forces supplied in Afghanistan. A £1.6 billion contract signed in May 2006 ensured that more Hercules were available for front line service. (*Courtesy* Camouflage *magazine*).

Private **Damian Wright** aged 23 from Mansfield and Private **Ben Ford** aged 18 from Chesterfield, both from the 2nd Battalion The Mercian Regiment (Worcesters and Foresters), were killed in Helmand Province, southern Afghanistan, on the morning of Wednesday 5 September 2007.

Senior Aircraftman **Christopher Bridge** aged 20, from Sheffield of C flight, 51 Squadron Royal Air Force Regiment was killed in Kandahar Province, southern Afghanistan on the morning of 30 August 2007.

Privates **Aaron James McClure** aged 19 from Ipswich, **Robert Graham Foster** aged 19 from Harlow and **John Thrumble** aged 21 from Chelmsford of 1st Battalion The Royal Anglian Regiment were killed after air support was called in during a fire fight with the Taliban and a bomb tragically struck the soldiers' position, north west of Kajaki, in northern Helmand Province on Thursday 23 August 2007.

Captain **David Hicks** aged 26 from Surrey of 1st Battalion The Royal Anglian Regiment was killed during an attack on his patrol base north-east of Sangin in Helmand Province on Saturday 11 August 2007.

Private **Tony Rawson** aged 27 from Dagenham, Essex of 1st Battalion The Royal Anglian Regiment was killed in southern Afghanistan on Friday 10 August 2007.

Lance Corporal **Michael Jones** aged 26 from Newbald, Yorkshire of Royal Marines was killed in action during operations in southern Afghanistan on Sunday 29 July 2007.

Sergeant **Barry Keen** aged 34 from Gateshead of 14 Signal Regiment was killed by a mortar attack in southern Afghanistan on Friday 27 July 2007.

Guardsman **David Atherton** aged 25 from Manchester of the 1st Battalion Grenadier Guards was killed in southern Afghanistan on Thursday 26 July 2007.

Lance Corporal **Alex Hawkins** aged 22 from East Dereham, Norfolk of 1st Battalion The Royal Anglian Regiment, was killed in southern Afghanistan on Wednesday 25 July 2007.

Guardsman **Daryl Hickey** aged 27 from Birmingham of the 1st Battalion Grenadier Guards was killed in southern Afghanistan on Thursday 12 July 2007. Gdsm Hickey was part of a fire team providing covering fire as others in his platoon assaulted a Taliban position.

Sergeant **Dave Wilkinson** aged 33 from Ashford, Kent of 19 Regiment Royal Artillery died following an explosion during a routine joint patrol with the Afghan National Army in Gereshk, Helmand province on Sunday 1 July 2007.

Captain **Sean Dolan** aged 40 from the West Midlands of 1st Battalion, The Worcestershire and Sherwood Foresters Regiment, died as a result of a mortar round in Helmand Province, Afghanistan, on Saturday 30 June 2007.

Drummer **Thomas Wright** aged 21 from Ripley, Derbyshire of 1st Battalion The Worcestershire and Sherwood Foresters Regiment, was killed on Sunday 24 June 2007 when the vehicle he was travelling in was caught in an explosion near Lashkar Gah, Helmand province.

Guardsman **Neil 'Tony' Downes** aged 20 from Manchester of 1st Battalion Grenadier Guards was killed on Saturday 9 June 2007 when his vehicle was hit by an explosion on a patrol with the Afghan National Army close to the town of Sangin in Helmand province, Afghanistan.

Lance Corporal **Paul 'Sandy' Sandford** aged 23 from Nottingham of 1st Battalion The Worcestershire and Sherwood Foresters, was killed while taking part in an offensive patrol with his company aimed at disrupting Taliban forces in the Upper Gereshk Valley area of Helmand Province on Wednesday 6 June 2007.

Corporal **Mike Gilyeat** aged 28 from Southport, Merseyside of the Royal Military Police, died on Wednesday 30 May 2007 when the American Chinook helicopter he was travelling in crashed in the Kajaki area of northern Helmand.

Corporal **Darren Bonner** aged 31 from Norfolk of the 1st Battalion The Royal Anglian Regiment died on Monday 28 May 2007, in Helmand Province, Afghanistan, as a result of an incident involving an explosive device.

Guardsman **Daniel Probyn** aged 22 from Tipton of 1st Battalion the Grenadier Guards died on Saturday 26 May 2007 following an overnight operation in Garmsir, southern Afghanistan.

Lance Corporal **George Russell Davey** aged 23 from Suffolk of 1st Battalion the Royal Anglian Regiment was killed on Sunday 20 May 2007 as a result of injuries sustained in a tragic accident at the British base in Sangin, Afghanistan.

Guardsman **Simon Davison** aged 22 from Newcastle-Upon-Tyne of 1st Battalion Grenadier Guards was killed by small arms fire in the town of Garmsir on Thursday 3 May 2007.

Private **Chris Gray** aged 19 from Leicestershire of 1st Battalion The Royal Anglian Regiment was killed in action whilst fighting the Taliban in Helmand Province, Afghanistan on Friday 13 April 2007.

Warrant Officer Class 2 **Michael Smith** aged 39 from Liverpool of 29 Commando Regiment Royal Artillery died from injuries sustained when a grenade was fired at the UK base in Sangin, Helmand Province, on Thursday 8 March 2007.

Marine **Benjamin Reddy** aged 22 from Ascot of 42 Commando Royal Marines was killed when his unit came under fire in the Kajaki area of Helmand Province on Tuesday 6 March 2007.

Lance Bombardier **Ross Clark** aged 25 from South Africa and Lance Bombardier **Liam McLaughlin** aged 21 from Lancashire, both of 29 Commando Regiment Royal Artillery, were killed during a rocket attack in the Sangin area of Helmand province on Saturday 3 March 2007.

Marine **Scott Summers** aged 23 from Crawley, East Sussex of 42 Commando Royal Marines died as a result of injuries sustained in a road traffic accident earlier that month in Afghanistan on Wednesday 21 February 2007.

Royal Marine **Jonathan Holland** aged 23 from Chorley in Lancashire of 45 Commando was killed by an anti-personnel mine during a routine patrol in the Sangin District of Helmand province on 21 February 2007.

Left: Swedish CV 90 armoured combat vehicle.

Below: Canadian Leopard being loaded on to a tank transporter bound for Kandahar.

The structure and 'internal workings' of a field hospital as deployed at Camp Bastion. (*Courtesy* Camouflage *magazine*)

Lance Corporal **Ford** aged 30 from Immingham, Lincolnshire of 45 Commando Royal Marines, died in Afghanistan on Monday 15 January 2007 when elements of 45 Commando Royal Marines were engaged in a deliberate offensive operation to the south of Garmsir in southern Helmand, Afghanistan.

Marine **Thomas Curry** aged 21 from East London of 42 Commando Royal Marines died on Saturday 13 January 2007 when elements of his commando were engaged in a deliberate offensive operation near Kajaki, in Northern Helmand, Afghanistan.

Lance Bombardier **James Dwyer** aged 22 from South Africa was killed when the vehicle he was driving struck an anti-tank mine whilst on a patrol in southern Helmand on Wednesday 27 December 2006.

Marine **Richard J. Watson** aged 23 from Caterham, Surrey of 42 Commando Royal Marines was killed on Tuesday 12 December 2006, in Now Zad, in the North of Helmand, Afghanistan.

Marine **Jonathan Wigley** aged 21 from Melton Mowbray, Leicestershire of 45 Commando Royal Marines died as a result of wounds sustained during an operation on the outskirts of the village of Garmsir, southern Helmand, on Tuesday 5 December 2006.

Marine **Gary Wright** aged 22 from Glasgow of 45 Commando Royal Marines died as a result of injuries sustained when a suicide-borne improvised explosive device detonated next to the vehicle in which he was patrolling in Lashkar Gah, Helmand Province, Afghanistan on 19 October 2006.

Lance Corporal **Paul Muirhead** aged 29 from Bearley, Warwickshire of 1 Royal Irish Regiment, who was very seriously injured during an attack by insurgents in northern Helmand Province on Friday 1 September 2006, died from his injuries on Wednesday 6 September 2006.

Lance Corporal **Luke McCulloch** aged 21 of 1 Royal Irish Regiment died as a result of a contact with insurgent forces in northern Helmand Province on Wednesday 6 September 2006.

Corporal **Mark William Wright** aged 27 from Edinburgh of 3rd Battalion, The Parachute Regiment was killed when a routine patrol encountered an unmarked minefield in the region of Kajaki, Helmand Province on Wednesday 6 September 2006.

Private **Craig O'Donnell** aged 24 from Clydebank of The Argyll and Sutherland Highlanders, 5th Battalion the Royal Regiment of Scotland was killed after the military convoy he was travelling in was attacked by a suspected suicide bomber in Kabul on Monday 4 September 2006.

Fourteen personnel were killed following the crash of a Nimrod MR2 aircraft on Saturday 2 September 2006. They were:

Flight Lieutenant **Steven Johnson** aged 38 from Collingham, Nottinghamshire

Flight Lieutenant **Leigh Anthony Mitchelmore** aged 28 from Bournemouth

Flight Lieutenant **Gareth Rodney Nicholas** aged 40 from Redruth, Cornwall

Flight Lieutenant **Allan James Squires** aged 39 from Clatterbridge

Flight Lieutenant **Steven Swarbrick** aged 28 from Liverpool

Flight Sergeant **Gary Wayne Andrews** aged 48 from Tankerton in Kent

Flight Sergeant **Stephen Beattie** aged 42 from Dundee

Flight Sergeant **Gerard Martin Bell**, aged 48 from Ely, Cambridgeshire

Flight Sergeant **Adrian Davies** aged 49 from Amersham, Buckinghamshire

Sergeant **Benjamin James Knight** aged 25 from Bridgwater

Sergeant **John Joseph Langton** aged 29 from Liverpool

Sergeant **Gary Paul Quilliam** aged 42 from Manchester

Corporal **Oliver Simon Dicketts** aged 27 from Wadhurst, Sussex

Marine **Joseph David Windall** aged 22 from Tylers Green, Buckinghamshire

Ranger **Anare Draiva** aged 27 from Fiji of 1 Royal Irish Regiment, died during a contact in Helmand Province at 1600 local time on Friday 1 September 2006.

Lance Corporal **Jonathan Peter Hetherington** aged 22 from South Wales of 14 Signal Regiment (Electronic Warfare) died following an attack on the Platoon House in Musa Qal'eh, northern Helmand Province on 27 August 2006.

Corporal **Bryan James Budd** aged 29 from Ripon of 3rd Battalion the Parachute Regiment was killed as a result of injuries sustained during a fire fight with Taliban forces in Sangin, Helmand Province, southern Afghanistan on Sunday 20 August 2006.

Lance Corporal **Sean Tansey** aged 26 from Washington, Tyne and Wear of The Life Guards was killed in an accident at a UK military base in Northern Helmand province on the afternoon of Saturday 12 August 2006.

Private **Leigh Reeves** aged 25 from Leicester of the Royal Logistics Corps was killed in a Road Traffic Accident at Camp Souter in Kabul on Wednesday 9 August 2006.

Private **Andrew Barrie Cutts** aged 19 from Mansfield of the Air Assault Support Regiment, Royal Logistic Corps was killed during operations against insurgent positions in Helmand Province on Sunday 6 August 2006.

Captain **Alex Eida** aged 29 from Surrey of the Royal Horse Artillery, Second Lieutenant **Ralph Johnson** aged 24 from Windsor of the Household Cavalry Regiment and Lance Corporal **Ross Nicholls** aged 27 from Edinburgh of the Blues and Royals were killed following an incident involving insurgent forces in northern Helmand Province on the morning of Tuesday 1 August 2006.

Private **Damien Jackson** aged 19 from South Shields, Tyne and Wear of 3rd Battalion the Parachute Regiment was killed in an incident involving insurgent forces on Wednesday 5 July 2006.

Corporal **Peter Thorpe** aged 27 from Barrow-in-Furness, Cumbria of the Royal Signals and Lance Corporal **Jabron Hashmi** aged 24 from Birmingham of the Intelligence Corps were killed following an incident in Sangin, Helmand Province, southern Afghanistan on 1 July 2006.

Australian LAV crew preparing
to move out.

Captain **David Patten** aged 38 of the Parachute Regiment and Sergeant **Paul Bartlett** aged 35 of the Royal Marines were killed on the morning of 27 June 2006 in Helmand Province.

Captain **Jim Philippson** aged 29 from St Albans in Hertfordshire of 7 Parachute Regiment Royal Horse Artillery died in Helmand Province, southern Afghanistan on the evening of Sunday 11 June 2006 when his mobile patrol was engaged in a firefight against suspected Taliban forces.

Lance Corporal **Peter Edward Craddock** aged 31 of 1st Battalion The Royal Gloucestershire, Berkshire and Wiltshire Regiment died as a result of a road traffic accident in Lashkar Gah, Afghanistan on Monday 27 March 2006.

Corporal **Mark Cridge** aged 25 of 7 Signal Regiment died in Camp Bastion, Afghanistan, on 22 March 2006.

Lance Corporal **Steven Sherwood** aged 23 from Ross-on-Wye, Herefordshire of the 1st Battalion, The Royal Gloucestershire, Berkshire and Wiltshire Light Infantry was killed on 29 October 2005, as a result of hostile action in Mazar-e-Sharif, Afghanistan. Five other members of Sherwood's patrol were injured when they came under fire.

Private **Jonathan Kitulagoda** aged 23 from Clifton, Bedfordshire of the Rifle Volunteers, TA, was killed, and four soldiers injured, by an apparent suicide bomb attack in Afghanistan on Wednesday 28 January 2004.

Sergeant **Robert Busuttil** and Corporal **John Gregory**, both aged 30 from the Royal Logistics Corps, died from gunshot wounds at the British base at Kabul International Airport, on 17 August 2002.

Private **Darren John George** aged 22 from Pirbright, Surrey of the Royal Anglian Regiment died on Tuesday 9 April 2002 following an incident during a security patrol in Kabul.

Military Fatalities in Afghanistan by Country

AUSTRALIA	11
BELGIUM	1
CANADA	132
CZECHOSLOVAKIA	3
DENMARK	30
ESTONIA	6
FINLAND	1
FRANCE	36
GERMANY	40
HUNGARY	2
ITALY	22
LATVIA	3

NETHERLANDS	21
NORWAY	5
POLAND	15
PORTUGAL	2
ROMANIA	11
SOUTH KOREA	2
SPAIN	26
SWEDEN	2
TURKEY	2
UK	237
USA	857
TOTAL	1,467

Abbreviations

AAA	Anti Aircraft Artillery
ABP	Afghan Border Patrol
ANA	Afghan National Army
ANP	Afghan National Police
ANSF	Afghan National Security Forces
AOO	Area of Operations
APC	Armoured Personnel Carrier
AQAM	Al-Qaeda Associated Movements
BDA	Battle Damage Assessment
C2	Command and Control
CAS	Close Air Support
CENTCOM	Central Command
CIA	Central Intelligence Agency
CIVCAS	Civilian Casualties
CN	Counter Narcotics
COB	Contingency Operating Base
COIN	Counter Insurgency
COMISAF	Commander ISAF
DoD	Department of Defense
EFP	Explosive Formed Penetrator
ETT	Embedded Training Team
FOB	Forward Operations Base
GIROA	Government of the Islamic Republic of Afghanistan
GPMG	General Purpose Machine Gun
HIG	Hezb-E Islami Gubuddin
HMG	Heavy Machine Gun

Clockwise from right:

A Rafale and Mirage 2000 of the Armée De L'air over Afghanistan. Such aircraft are greatly valued by ISAF as they know that the Taliban fear them.

During the Vietnam War the US A1E Skyraider was a superb aircraft for COIN operations, and plans are currently in place to find a modern-day equivalent for service in Afghanistan.

A British TA soldier mentors an Afghan soldier shortly before an operation against Taliban insurgents.

Royal Marine GPMG gunner in Helmand.

An ISAF PRT medical team going about its greatly valued business in an Afghan village. Just looking at the turnout you can see how important their service is.

General Stanley McChrystal, Commander ISAF and Commander USFOR-A.

British WMIK riding shot gun for supply convoy in Helmand.

USMC AV8 Harrier at Kandahar.

HQN	Haqqani Network
IED	Improvised Explosive Device
INS	Insurgents
ISAF	International Security Assistance Force
ISI	Inter-Services Intelligence
ISR	Intelligence Surveillance and Reconnaissance
JDAM	Joint Direct Attack Munition
JTAC	Joint Tactical Air Controllers
MANPADS	Man Portable Air Defence System
MSR	Main Supply Route
NATO	North Atlantic Treaty Organization
OPCOM	Operational Command
OPLAN	Operational Plan
OPSEC	Operational Security
OPTAG	Operational Training Advisory Group
PRT	Provincial Reconstruction Team
QST	Quetta Shura Taliban
ROE	Rules of Engagement
RPG	Rocket propelled Grenade
RSTA	Reconnaissance Surveillance Target Acquisition
SACEUR	Supreme Allied Commander Europe
SAM	Surface to Air Missile
SAW	Squad Assault Weapon
SF	Special Forces
SHAPE	Supreme Headquarters Allied Powers Europe
SOF	Special Operations Forces
SOG	Special Operations Group
SOP	Standard Operational Procedures
TACOM	Tactical Command
UAV	Unmanned Air Vehicle
UCAV	Unmanned Combat Air Vehicle
USFOR-A	US Forces Afghanistan
USMC	United States Marine Corps

AFTERWORD

By Myrdal Mya, an Afghani serving with the Canadian Cadet Forces

Looking at the issues in Afghanistan, no simple solution pops into my mind. There are many things to be considered including the past of the Afghani people, the perception of Afghani people and the implications of military presence in Afghanistan.

The Afghan people strongly believe in their way of living. Their wartime struggles in the past have given them a sense of being able to survive without foreign influences or modern advances in technology. They have staved off invasion throughout history and have managed to survive despite many perceived shortcomings. They have survived without the influence of others; this gives the Afghani people something to hang their hat on, something that they can build upon. The past is littered with building blocks that have allowed the Afghan people to form a barrier to shield them from others around them.

The priorities of the Afghani people and the foreign military differ greatly, which can be the cause for disconnect between the military support and the people of Afghanistan. The main concern for most families is surviving the daily struggles of life in an impoverished nation. They recognize the presence of foreigners as a path to get rid of the Taliban that has been oppressing them for many years. But to the Afghan people, the effort needed to create this change in their country isn't worth the end result when they are struggling to satisfy their basic needs. They are far more concerned with where their next meal will come from, or the next time they will have fresh water and until the priorities of the two parties become convergent there will be little progress.

There is often talk about building infrastructure to help get Afghanistan on its feet, but due to the beleaguered past of the Afghani people, they can't see

US Marines maintaining a ground presence in an Afghan village. How long will they be there?

Soldiers from the Royal Scots dive for cover after coming under fire from a mosque that they were visiting. The Taliban militants who ambushed them escaped by means of motorbikes parked nearby, taking advantage of the fact that the British troops could not fire on them for fear of hitting innocent civilians.

Soldiers from 2 Para proudly march through the streets of Colchester following their return from Afghanistan. Such scenes are becoming increasingly popular in the UK as the public wish to show their admiration and support for our service personnel if not for the actual cause itself.

the potential for positive impact that the changes brought about by the foreign military presence may bring. They are blinded by the pride in their way of life, not being able to see beyond the immediate future. If the foreign military in Afghanistan can improve the quality of living of the Afghani people without sacrificing their way of life then the Afghani people might be more willing to take part in the rebuilding of their nation. Let us be clear; Afghanistan does not want to be become a westernized nation, even if this means that their quality of life may significantly increase. A personal example may give insight into the way the Afghani people think.

In 2001, my grandmother was very ill and the level of medical care in Afghanistan was making her life more painful. Her life was slowly coming to an end and this woman, who even in her old age was still very caring and intelligent, had no idea what was best for her. My parents had made mention of the idea of her coming to live with us in Canada so that she could get better health care and live the rest of her days with less pain. She instantly refused, claiming that she had a great life and that she didn't want to leave. She passed away in 2003 and at that time, my parents blamed themselves. We couldn't understand why she would choose to live in such an impoverished and oppressed country, but we came to realize that we had spent too much time outside of Afghanistan and had become disillusioned as to the reality of living in Afghanistan. The people there have become accustomed to the way of life they have, and the thought of other countries providing a better life is absurd. If I, someone who has lived in Afghanistan, can lose touch with the Afghani way of life, how can the foreign military be expected to make Afghanistan a better place to live?

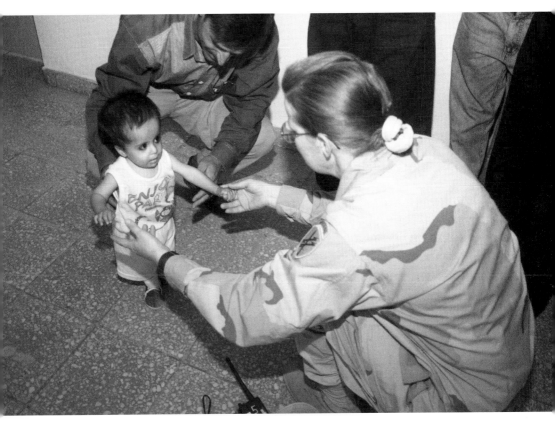

ISAF Medic at work.

Afghans registering to vote in the 2009 elections.

This page: Sometimes you just cannot beat the Mk I donkey for utility and
go-anywhere capability.

Opposite, clockwise from top: Air drop, FOB; British work-up training on Salisbury
Plain; 'heck, I'm in a foreign country'; unexploded mortar round; ordnance destruction.

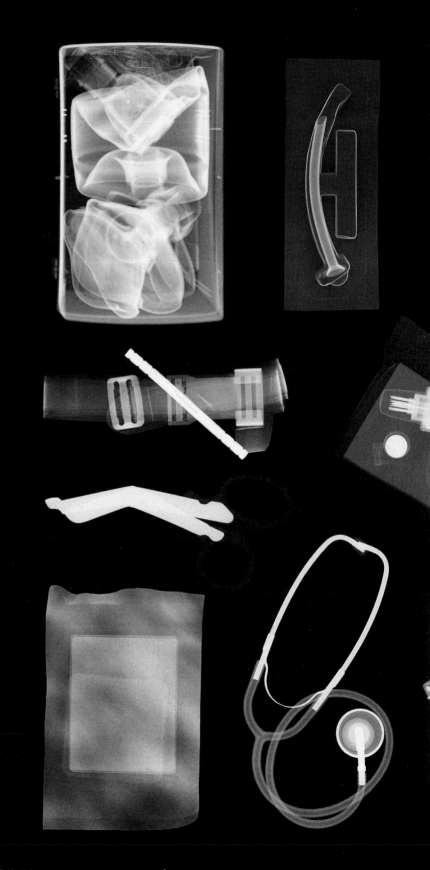

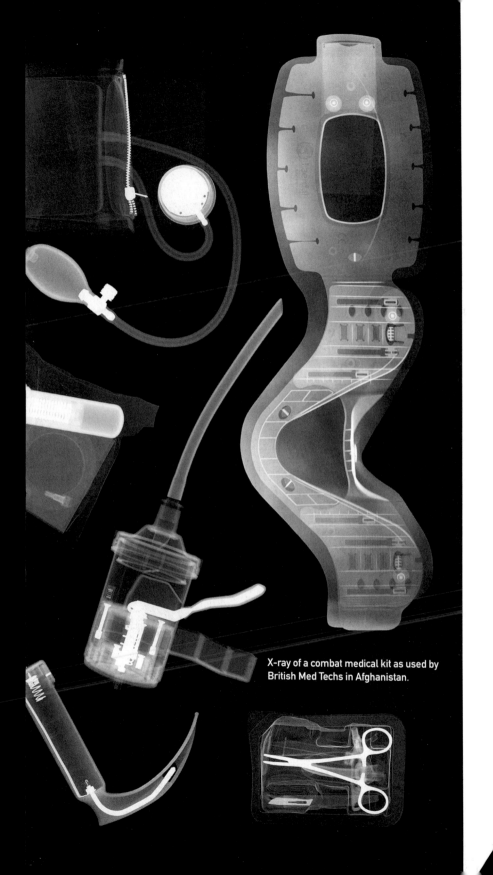

X-ray of a combat medical kit as used by British Med Techs in Afghanistan.

INDEX

A10 36, 140

Abdullah, Dr Abdullah 101

AGM-114 Hellfire 61

AIM 9 Sidewinder 61

ANA 14, 17, 22, 36, 52, 93–4, 117, 120, 133, 157, 168–9, 172–3

ANAAC 172

ANP 22, 52, 93, 97, 100, 120, 157, 168–9, 172–3

AQT 26

Afghan Border 29

Afghan Elections 14, 17, 36, 101, 217

Afghan Government 16, 21, 148, 153

Afghan National Security Forces 145, 148, 152, 160, 164, 169, 172

Afghan People 32, 89, 101, 105, 109, 144–5, 213, 216

Afghan Public Protection Force 173

Air Strikes 65

Al-Qaeda 13, 16–17, 20, 25, 30–1, 40, 60, 89, 92, 152, 176–7

Apache Helicopters 136

Arbuthnot, James 85

Artillery Barrages 65

Asif Ali Zardari 16, 40

Asymmetric Warfare 176

Australian Gunners 37

BERPS 46

Ballistic Eye Protection 72

Bajaur Region 29

Battlefield Afghanistan 12, 32, 77

Battlefields of Afghanistan 69

Bhutto, Benazir 30

Bin Laden, Osama 21, 25, 92

Black Hawk Helicopters 84–5, 136

Watch 113, 132, 136–7, 141

uth Waziristan 29

British Government 81

Brown, Gordon 16, 20

Brownout 41, 44, 46

Bush, George W. 16

CASEVAC 72

CIA 21, 31, 60, 92

CIA SOG 21

COB 72

COIN 109, 144–5, 153, 156, 165, 169, 172

Camp Bastion 69

Canada 88–9

Chinese Rockets 37, 41, 183

Chinook 40–1, 44, 69, 88, 128, 132–3, 136, 140

Civilian Casualties 20

Combat Medicine 69

Cougar 49, 57, 59

Creech AFB 61

Critical Care Air Transport Team 72

Crucible for Terrorism 16

Dannatt, General Sir Richard 84

DARPA 74

DEA 45

Danish Battle Group 121, 132

Danish Leopard Tanks 37

Death of British soldiers at hands of Afghan police officer 100

Devil's Chariots 32

Drug Trafficking 21

EFPs 56

FOB 64, 80, 112, 116, 123, 126, 179, 219

Fixed Wing Losses 45

Force Protection Vehicles 52

Focused District Development 172

Focused Ultrasound 72

Fortified villages 105

Forward Surgical Team 72

GBU-12 Paveway LGB 61

GBU-JDAM 61

General Atomics MQ-9 Reaper 60